EDITOR: LEE JOHNSON

OSPREY MILITARY

MEN-AT-ARMS SERIES | 283

EARLY ROMAN ARMIES

Text by
NICK SEKUNDA & SIMON NORTHWOOD
Colour plates by
RICHARD HOOK

First published in Great Britain in 1995 by
Osprey, an imprint of Reed Consumer Books Ltd.
Michelin House, 81 Fulham Road,
London SW3 6RB
and Auckland, Melbourne, Singapore and Toronto

ISBN 1 85532 513 6

Filmset in Great Britain
Printed through World Print Ltd, Hong Kong

Acknowledgments

The authors would like to thank Dr. J. Briscoe and Mr.
T.J. Quinn for their help in the writing of this book.
They would also like to express a debt of gratitude to
Peter Connolly, whose book *Greece and Rome at War*,
which constituted the first attempt to integrate the
historical and archaeological evidence dealing with the
army of Archaic Rome, has been a constant source of
reference.

Publisher's note

Readers may wish to study this title in conjunction with
the following Osprey publications:

    MAA   46 *The Roman Army from Caesar to Trajan*
    MAA 121 *Armies of the Carthaginian Wars 265–146 BC*
    Campaign 36 *Cannae 216 BC*

Artist's note

Readers may care to note that the original paintings
from which the colour plates in this book were pre-
pared are available for private sale. All reproduction
copyright whatsoever is retained by the publisher. All
enquiries should be addressed to:

    Scorpio Gallery
    PO Box 475
    Hailsham
    E. Sussex BN27 2SL

The publishers regret that they can enter into no
correspondence upon this matter.

ROME'S EARLY HISTORY

Early Rome and the Romans were only one of a number of peoples and settlements in Iron Age Italy. From the earliest historical times Rome fell under the influence of her powerful Etruscan neighbours to the north, and, indeed, throughout most of the sixth century BC Rome was ruled by kings, the Tarquins, who came originally from the Etruscan city of Tarquinii. In 509 (according to later Roman tradition) the last of these Etruscan kings, Tarquinius Superbus, was expelled. Rome declared herself a Republic, and was governed by two annually elected magistrates known as 'consuls'. For a while, how–

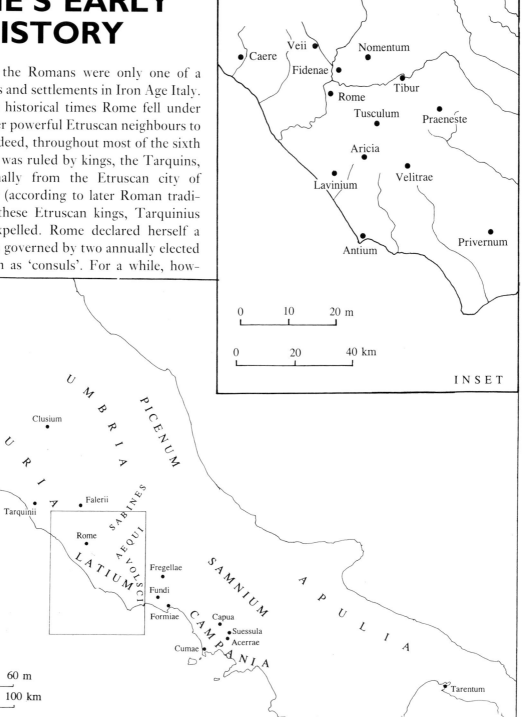

INSET

3

ever, Rome fell under the control of Lars Porsenna of Clusium. Porsenna was defeated at Aricia in *c.* 504 by an alliance between Rome, other Latin peoples and Aristodemus of Cumae. However, Rome was left in a weakened position and the Latins refused to accept Roman hegemony instead embarking on a war against her. This ended with a Roman victory at Lake Regillus (variously 499 or 496), but, although Rome was victorious, the settlement with the Latins, known as the Cassian treaty, seems to have been more of a compromise than a return to the previous situation of Roman dominance.

Latium at this time was increasingly threatened by a number of Apennine hill tribes. A common defensive alliance was agreed which aimed at presenting a united front against them. How the alliance worked in practice is difficult to tell given the scarcity and unreliability of our historical source material. All the Latin communities, including Rome, will have provided troops, but who commanded them? One literary fragment from the first century BC Roman antiquarian Cincius implies an annual command rotating between the various members of the alliance. Much of the fifth century BC saw Rome at war alongside the Latins defending Latium against the Sabines, Volsci and Aequi who were eager to settle in more fertile territory. In this endeavour the alliance seems to have been largely successful and in the later part of the century former territorial losses were being recovered.

Not all Roman warfare was organized as part of the Latin alliance. The security of Rome's northern border was essentially her own responsibility, and this involved protection against the closest Etruscan city, Veii, which was situated twelve miles north-east of Rome on the opposite bank of the Tiber. Rome was at war with Veii in 483–474 (during which time there occurred a famous Roman defeat at the battle of

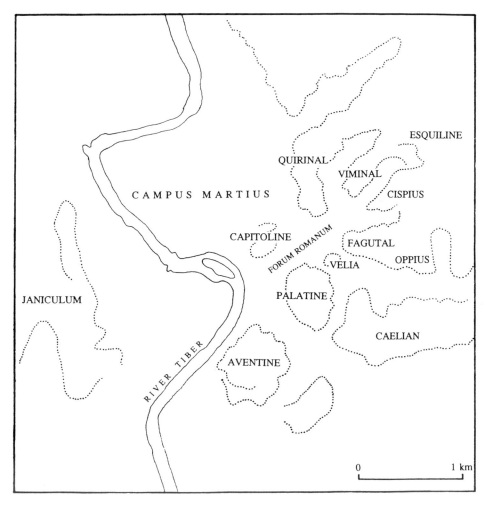

At Rome the River Tiber has cut a deep valley into the local tufa rock about a mile across. Some of the hills of Rome, the Capitoline, the Palatine and Aventine, lie in this valley separated from its sides, while others, the Caelian, Oppian, Esquiline, Viminal and Quirinal, are spurs connected to the valley sides. The Tiber flows in two loops, the northern one containing the marshy Campus Martius.

Cremera). Conflict began again intermittently in the 430s until the Veientine satellite colony of Fidenae was destroyed in 426. The most important conflict with Veii, however, began in 406 and lasted for ten years, at the end of which Veii was conquered by the Roman general Camillus. Veii was destroyed and her territory seized. This was a most significant development since it was the first time Rome had destroyed and occupied an enemy state of comparable size.

Rome's expansion was temporarily halted by the Gallic incursion of Brennus, during which the city of Rome was sacked following a crushing defeat at the Allia (traditional date 390 BC). Rome's long term position seems not to have been unduly damaged, however. Indeed an extended period of aggression, which had begun with the war against Veii, continued with the recapture of the Pomptine district of Latium from the Volsci and the annexation of the nearby Latin community of Tusculum in 381.

Rome's next major wars were undertaken against the Latin towns of Tibur and Praeneste. These had never been part of the Latin League allied to Rome, but they now posed a threat to Roman dominance in Latium, perhaps as champions of the Latins against Rome. Both towns were finally defeated in 354. Shortly afterwards concurrent wars in Etruria reached a successful conclusion: forty year truces were granted to Caere in 353 and to Tarquinii and Falerii in 351.

Rome now had no serious challenger in Latium and possessed a secure northern border with Etruria. Her next entanglements were to draw her into operations in new theatres. In 343 the peoples of Campania appealed to Rome for help against the Samnites, a powerful group of tribes who inhabited the central southern highlands of Italy. Rome intervened on behalf of the Campanians and the conflict was concluded in 341.

That same year the Latins finally rebelled against Rome and united themselves with the Volsci. This was a serious rebellion but it was suppressed by 338, in which year the Romans fundamentally reformed their relationship with the Latins and their other allies. Many communities lost their independence and became *municipia* with Roman citizenship; others negotiated new treaties with Rome and still others received a new status (the *civitas sine suffragio* or 'citizenship without the vote') which imposed all

Ornamental shield from Esquiline Tomb 94. This shield was probably manufactured in Etruria, possibly in Tarquinia which was a major manufacturing centre. Like other Etruscan 'Parade-Shields' of this period, the Esquiline shield was of extremely thin sheet bronze, decorated with repoussé ornamentation. Consequently it has survived only in an extremely fragmentary condition, and so a reconstruction drawing has been shown. These 'Parade-Shields' were presumably funerary versions of more robust shields which were actually used in combat. The original diameter was something like 61 cm. Note the central handle and the four or five terminals attached by staples to the inside of the shield. These may have been for the attachment of straps which would enable the shield to be worn on the back when not in use.

the responsibilities of Roman citizenship (military service and payment of taxes) but did not allow office-holding or participation in elections at Rome.

Having thus strengthened her position, Rome established colonies in Campania and the Liris valley and in 326 entered into an alliance with Neapolis: all moves which angered the Samnites and precipitated the Second Samnite War. This began in 326 and was pursued for over twenty years, despite even the humiliating Roman defeat at the Caudine forks in 321 where a double consular army was captured by the Samnites. The war ended, however, in 304 with the Samnites ceding control of the Liris valley.

The Third Samnite War began in 298. In a final bid to secure their independence the Samnites organized a grand alliance of Samnites, Etruscans, Celts and Umbrians. The seriousness for Rome was obvious, but the Romans were able to defeat their enemies piecemeal, their most notable victories being against the Samnites and Gauls at Sentinum in 295 and Apulonia in 293. Defeat of the Samnite-led coalition, completed in 290, gave Rome effective control over all the native Italian peoples south of the Po valley. Now only the Greek coastal cities of South Italy remained free.

In 282 Rome sent a garrison to Thurii in response to a request for aid against her marauding Lucanian neighbours. The people of Tarantum regarded this as interference within their sphere of influence and appealed for aid to their fellow Greek, King Pyrrhus of Epirus. Pyrrhus landed in Italy in 280 and won two 'Pyrrhic' victories at Heraclea and Asculum but was finally defeated in 275 and forced to leave Italy. Rome's dominance was now beyond challenge.

For most of this period the literary sources at our disposal are of lamentable quality. Our principal sources are Livy and Dionysius of Halicarnassus, who both worked at Rome during the reign of the Emperor Augustus (31 BC–AD 14). In fact the ancient accounts of the history of Rome only become truly reliable when Pyrrhus comes onto the scene. The campaigns of Pyrrhus were described by earlier Greek historians, some of whom, like Pyrrhus' court historian Proxenos, and indeed Pyrrhus himself,

actually witnessed the events described. Thus the descriptions of the Roman army contained in surviving accounts of the war with Pyrrhus can be regarded as reliable. All information concerning the Roman army in particular, and Roman history in general before this date is unreliable.

Rome only started to produce her own native historians towards the end of the third century. These are known to modern historians as the 'annalists'. The only reliable information they had available to draw on for the early history of Rome were lists of magistrates and treaties of alliance, otherwise they had to use mythology and oral tradition. Livy and Dionysius relied heavily on the 'annalists' and thus though their works are unreliable as a whole, they occasionally contain 'nuggets' of information which seem to reflect accurate and genuine tradition. The task of the modern military historian is to sift out these nuggets from the slurry wherein they float. Needless to say, there is little which can be written on this period with absolute certainty.

Any study of the Roman army within this period falls naturally into three sections dealing with the pre-hoplite army, the hoplite army, and the manipular army.

Etruscan statuette of a warrior on a candelabrum from the 'Circolo del Tritone', Vetulonia, now in Florence. The decoration on the back of the shield indicates that the warrior carries a more robust version of the 'Etruscan Parade Shield' which was actually used in combat.

The fact that the warrior carries the shield suspended from his shoulders, presumably to allow him to throw his spear, shows that the attachments on the back of the 'Parade Shield' were designed for attachment to straps. He also carries a mace in his left hand.

Left: This 'Calotte' helmet from Esquiline Tomb 94, now in the Capitoline Museum, has been dated to the first half of the seventh century. This early photograph demonstrates the fragmentary state of the skull: it is possible that the helmet originally had a number of plume and other fittings which were not recovered during excavation.

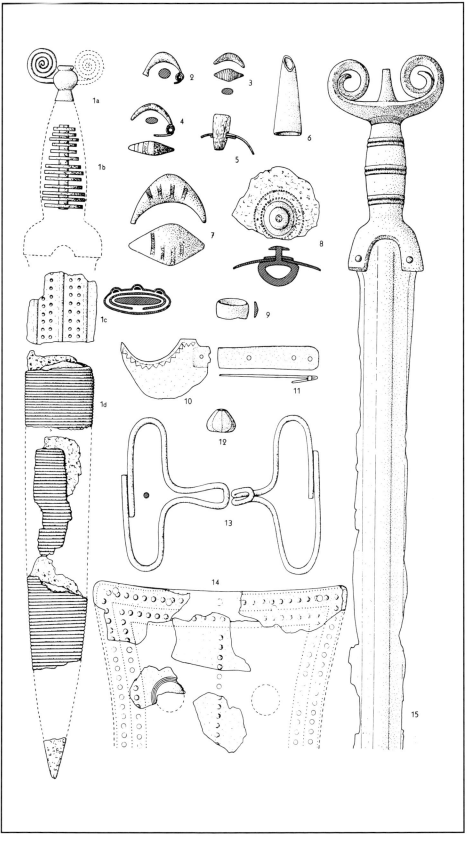

Findgroup 98 from the Esquiline, from a warrior-burial, excavated in the Via Giovanni Lanza. The short sword (1), found in a fragmentary condition, had an iron blade and a bronze pommel. The scabbard would have been wood, partially faced with an embossed bronze plate at top, and bound with a bronze wire. The bronze butt (6) has survived from the warrior's spear, but the iron spearhead had completely disappeared. The iron disk (8) may have been a boss from a wooden shield, though this is uncertain. The warrior's panoply was completed by a bronze pectoral (14) which also only survived in a fragmentary state. Also shown are brooches (fibulae, 2–4, 7), used to secure the cloak and tunic, a bronze 'razor' or whittling-knife (10–11) and a belt-buckle (13).

THE PRE-HOPLITE ARMY

Traditionally Rome was founded in 753 BC by the twin brothers Romulus and Remus, sons of the god Mars, who had been suckled in infancy by a she-wolf. In fact the city of Rome first came into existence when separate communities on the Palatine and Quirinal hills amalgamated some time around 600 BC. The legend of Romulus and Remus only emerged during the fourth century under the influence of Greek writers. If there is any truth at all in the legend of the twins, one of whom had to die in order for a unified Roman people to emerge, it may be that two communities had to amalgamate to form Rome.

Warrior-burials on the Esquiline Hill

The earliest preserved remains from Rome date from the eighth and ninth centuries BC. At this time the huts of the village which would eventually become the Eternal City lay on the Capitoline Hill, while the necropolis of the settlement was situated on the Esquiline Hill. A number of early tombs there were excavated in 1885 during construction work on a

housing project. Of these tombs, some are clearly 'warrior-burials', while others contain assorted weapons. It is from these finds that we can form an image of the appearance of the earliest Roman warriors (*see* Plate A).

Only two helmets have emerged from early Rome, and both are of the 'Calotte' type, though it is possible that other helmet types were used too. The standard form of body-protection was the 'pectoral' or breastplate, of which some three have survived. They are rectangular in shape, with incurving sides, a little less than 20 cm wide and a little more than 20 cm long. Presumably they were worn with the long side running vertically, though this is not certain. The smaller sides are pierced with holes for the attachment of a leather backing and straps to hold the pectoral in place. The precise way in which these straps ran round the shoulders is unknown. The pectorals are decorated with bands of geometric ornamentation round the edge, and five bosses, one in the centre and one in each of the four corners.

One large ornamental bronze shield has survived. This shield is entirely Etruscan in style, and may well have been manufactured in one of the major manufacturing centres of Etruria, such as Tarquinii. We should also note, however, that an iron boss found separately might have come from a wooden shield. Two sizes of sword have been recovered, short swords about 44 cm long, and long swords about 70 cm long. The latter generally have an 'antenna' hilt. Sword blades at this time were generally bronze, but iron examples are occasionally found. Numerous spear-heads have been found in the Esquiline Tombs, sometimes of iron, sometimes of bronze. They have leaf-shaped blades and typically a multi-faceted central section, sometimes decorated with a geometric pattern.

Roman sardonyx gem showing two bearded Salii priests. (Photo: Staatliche Museen zu Berlin)

The Salii

Down to the end of the Republic and well into the imperial period there existed at Rome two colleges of 'Salii', the priests of Mars. The cult of the *Salii Palatini* was connected with Mars and, according to tradition, with an ancient miraculous shield called an *ancile*. The *Salii Collini* was connected with Quirinus. Quirinus was the Sabine name for Mars, and was derived from the Sabine word for lance. Consequently we can be confident that two separate colleges of the Salii existed before the coalescence of the two separate communities on the Palatine and Quirinal hills around 600 BC. Many of the Republican institutions of Rome indicate that the early city incorporated both Latin and Sabine elements within its population.

Both colleges of priests were dedicated to the war-god, and many of the martial features of the institution of the Salii suggest that their origin lay in warrior bands bound by oath to serve the war-god. Each of the two colleges consisted of 12 life-members from patrician families, both of whose parents were required to be still living. This was presumably initially an injunction of military significance: the head of a family could not be a member of the Salii lest he should lose his life in battle. It may also indicate that at this early period the main social division between plebeian and patrician had military significance: only the patricians were rich enough to provide themselves with weapons, and were therefore able to participate in warfare. At the head of each college was a *magister*. The term *magister* is of military origin, denoting a magistracy or military command in Etruscan inscriptions.

It was a feature of most ancient communities that when new military or political institutions of the citizenry were established, they were placed under the protection of a particular deity. Worship was offered to the deity to ensure the survival and pros-

Below right: Raymond Bloch has suggested that this cornelian intaglio, present whereabouts unknown, shows two warriors rather than Salii, carrying five ancilia hung on a pole. The first warrior, however, seems to carry an apex in his hand. The seal dates to the fourth or third century BC; note the crested Italo-Attic helmets and muscle-cuirasses.

Right and below: Agate intaglio in the Archaeological Museum, Florence, showing two Salian priests moving the ancilia. It is inscribed, in Etruscan though the name is Latin, Appius alce 'Appius gave'.

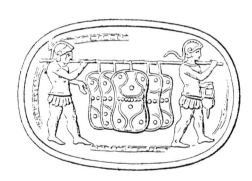

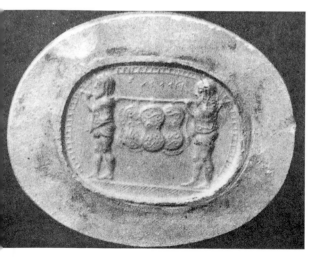

perity of that institution. In the course of time it would be necessary to reorganize the citizen body and establish new civic and military institutions. When this happened, however, the original institution frequently continued a shadowy existence as a social 'fossil', obsolete in any meaningful way, but continuing as a religious college which met to maintain the established acts of worship. Failure to maintain the established rites would constitute a sacrilegious act, and would be sure to bring down the wrath of the slighted god onto the community. In the priestly colleges of the Salii we seem to have such a fossil.

Some features of the institution of the Salii may therefore reflect Roman military practices before the institution of the tribal system. It may be that only young patricians participated in warfare, and only then if they were not heads of families. They formed themselves into warrior-bands, perhaps restricted to twelve men, who dedicated themselves to the worship of Mars in return for that god's support in battle. Needless to say, this is all highly speculative. Similar colleges of Salii existed in other Latin cities such as Aricia, Alba, Lavinium, Tusculum, Tibur and Anagnia. So this form of warfare seems to have been general in Latium, and not restricted to Rome.

Salian dress and equipment

The dress and equipment of the Salii are described by Livy, Dionysius of Halicarnassus and Plutarch. They wore a decorated many-coloured tunic, purple according to Plutarch, and what Livy calls 'a bronze covering for the chest'. These breastplates may correspond to the square pectorals recovered from the Esquiline tombs discussed above. Over the tunic was worn a *trabea* cloak described by Dionysius. His words are difficult to interpret, but he seems to say that they were striped in scarlet, bordered in purple and fastened with a brooch. Plutarch adds that they wore bronze belts and helmets and carried short daggers, while Dionysius tells us that they carried short spears or staffs.

The most distinctive item associated with the Salii was the *ancile*. The *ancile* was an oval shiel made of bronze and decorated with relief work on th outside. The sides of these shields were indented This rough 'figure-of-eight' shape has led to sugges tions that the shield may have ultimately derive from Mycenaean prototypes, but the shape is s common in all areas at all times that a local Italia origin is to be preferred. No actual *ancilia* or shield of a comparable shape have survived, but sma bronze votive shields of this shape have been re covered in archaeological contexts in Picenum an adjacent regions dating to 700 BC and later. Thus seems possible to suggest that use of the *ancile* sprea across the Apennines into Latium during the sevent century BC prior to the introduction of hoplite equip ment and tactics. The actual origin of the *ancile*, a opposed to that in Roman tradition, is obscure. The may originally have been shields routinely used i battle by Roman warriors, or, less probably, boot captured from the enemy at some point in the past.

One further distinctive feature of the Salii wa their pointed helmet, called an *apex*. An actual ex ample of a Salian *apex* has been recovered in a lat Republican context. It is made in silver, and so doe not directly reflect an ancient helmet type, though probably preserves an approximate representation c the shape of such an early helmet. Perhaps only th side ribs, brow-band and studs were metal in th

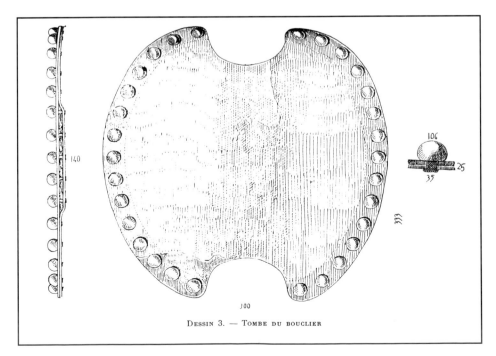

DESSIN 3. — TOMBE DU BOUCLIER

French archaeological excavations in the region of Bolsena revealed a warrior tomb, called by the excavator 'Tombe du Bouclier' after this bronze miniature (335×305 mm) shield, slightly oval in shape. The distinctive cut-out sections in the sides led the excavator to identify this type of shield as the ancestor of the ancilia later carried by the Salii.

riginal apex helmet, while the cap beneath them may have been leather. Perhaps the olive-wood spike t the top of the helmet may be the descendant of a ooden crest-holder.

The tribal system

he earliest possibly reliable information concerning he size and organization of the earliest Roman rmy describes how it was recruited from three ribes'. Roman society was at some early stage ivided into three tribes and thirty *curiae*. The word *uria* is generally derived from *co-viria*, that is, 'an ssembly of armed men'. The *curiae* formed the oting units of the earliest Roman assembly, the *omitia curiata*. Each *curia* was formed from a umber of families (*gentes*) and ten of these *curiae* ormed a tribe (*tribus*). That there were indeed origi- ally three tribes is confirmed by the etymology of *ribus* which was derived from *tris* (the Latin for three') and literally meant 'divided into three'. Each ribe appears to have been commanded by a *tribunus ilitum* and to have contributed 1,000 men (i.e. 100 rom each *curia*). This led the Roman antiquarian 'arro to speculate that *miles* (the Latin for 'soldier')

he internal handle rrangements of the ancile re unknown. Hellenistic tatues of Juno Sospita how handle arrangements imilar to those for a oplite shield, but they nay have entered the epresentational canon nder Greek influence, and perhaps do not represent seventh century reality. The inside of an ancile and an ornamental Salian dagger are shown on this example of a Roman aes grave coin, though such coins have been dismissed as forgeries.

was derived from *mille* (the Latin for 'a thousand'): 'soldiers are *milites* because at first the legion was made of three thousand and each of the individual tribes of Tities, Ramnes and Luceres sent a thousand soldiers'. Although Varro's etymology is probably incorrect (the true etymology of *miles* is unknown), the fact that he was able to suggest such an interpretation demonstrates that the tradition that each tribe contributed a thousand men to the legion was already well established when he wrote.

The horsemen in this organization are said to have been divided into three groups each of 100 men. Livy and Cicero tell us that these groups had the names Ramnes, Tities and Luceres, names which Varro said applied to the whole tribe. This should not worry us unduly – the longer survival of this early cavalry organization meant that these names were later associated only with the cavalry. It is unclear whether these cavalry are the same as the 300 *celeres* (literally 'the swift') who were supposedly instituted by Rome's first and legendary king, Romulus, as a bodyguard (*see* Livy, Festus, and Servius).

Exactly what these 'horsemen' were is obscure. True cavalry may not have existed at this time, and we can perhaps compare conditions in archaic Greece. Here the title of *hippeis* was given to élite

bands of hoplites who no longer used horses in batt but had originally used chariots, then horses, as means of travelling to the battlefield and as an indica tion of their social status. Thus the Roman *equites* the fifth century may have no more been horseme than the Spartan *hippeis* of the same period.

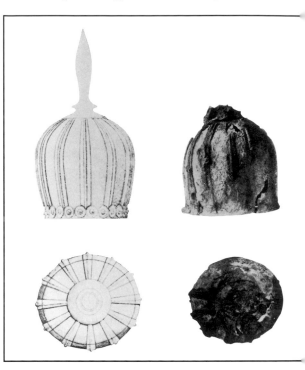

Above: Silver apex *helmet once belonging to one of the* Salii, *recovered from water-reservoir beneath the* atrium *of the Domus Augustana on the Palatine This presumably preserve the shape of a more practical archaic helmet, perhaps in leather with metal ribs and brim.*

The principal emblem of the Flamen *priest was his white pointed hat (*apex*) made from the hide of a sacrificed animal. The point was made of olive wood. The* flamines *were expected to wear this hat at all times when out of doors. This detail from th* Ara Pacis Augustae *shows two* flamines *wearing* ape *headgear.*

Tradition claims that the tribal system was introduced by Romulus in the eighth century BC. But modern historians are unanimous in concluding that this cannot be the case. The three tribal names (Tities, Ramnes and Luceres) are clearly Etruscan. Consequently the system of three tribes and thirty *curiae* was introduced under the direct influence of the Etruscans, probably towards the end of the seventh century BC. This immediately raises the much larger problem of which method of warfare and equipment was used by the three tribes. It is possible that hoplite tactics and equipment were introduced at Rome at the same time as the tribal system, i.e. a little before 600 BC; but it is more probable that they were introduced some half-century later by Servius Tullius.

THE HOPLITE ARMY

Hoplite tactics were developed in Greece *c.* 675 BC and reached Etruria *c.* 600 BC, where their use is confirmed in a wide variety of contemporary artwork. Dionysius of Halicarnassus reports how the Etruscan towns of Falerii and Fescennium preserved hoplite equipment, despite being colonized by Romans: 'Falerii and Fescennium were even down to my day inhabited by Romans . . . in these cities there survived many ancient customs which the Greeks had once used, such as their type of weaponry: Argolic shields and spears'.

From Etruria this new form of warfare spread to Rome and to the other Latins. This fact is well established in the ancient tradition: 'In ancient times, when the Romans used rectangular shields, the Etruscans fought in phalanx using bronze shields, but having compelled the Romans to adopt the same equipment they were themselves defeated' (Diodorus). 'The Romans took close battle formation from the Etruscans, who used to attack in a phalanx' (Athenaeus). 'The Etruscans did not fight in maniples but made war on us armed with bronze shields in a phalanx; we were re-armed and adopting the equipment of the enemy we formed up against them; and in this way we were able to conquer even those most accustomed to fighting in phalanx' (*Ineditum Vaticanum*). Even Livy knew this, remarking that before the introduction of military pay the Romans had employed the round shield in a Macedonian style phalanx.

These two terracottas from Veii, produced at the beginning of the fifth century, show a pair of naked young men engaged in a war-dance. As in ancient Greece, the war dance was a survival of pre-hoplite warfare; its steps were designed to train the young warrior in the moves employed in single combat. One of the dancers carries a hoplite shield, while the other carries a square shield. The appearance of the square shield is difficult to interpret, but perhaps implies that when Rome was using hoplite methods of warfare not all other Latin cities followed suit, which is indicated in some literary sources. Both figurines would originally have had miniature spears in their right hands. (Photo: Museo Nazionale di Villa Giulia, Rome)

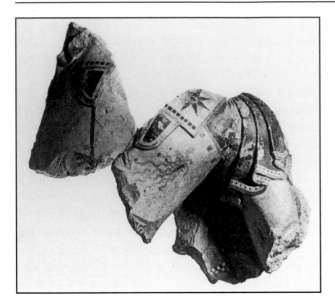

Painted terracotta body of an Amazon, dating to the early years of the fifth century, from the pediment of a temple on the Esquiline. The principal colour is sometimes stated to be black, but reproductions show a dark navy blue. It is by Greek artists, perhaps Damophilus and Gorgasus, known to have been active in Rome at the same period. Clearly this sculpture is of a mythological subject, even though wearing hoplite equipment, and so cannot be taken as evidence for the adoption of hoplite equipment and even less so for hoplite tactics by the Roman army. (Photo: Soprintendenza Archeologica di Roma)

The introduction of hoplite tactics to Rome is associated in Roman historical tradition with the penultimate king of Rome, Servius Tullius (traditional dates 578–534 BC). Servius was said to have introduced a sweeping reform which changed the prevailing social order divided by *gens* and *curia* which we have already described. The most important innovation was that citizenship by race was replaced by one based on residence, thus perhaps increasing the pool of military manpower. These newly defined citizens were subject to the *census* in which their wealth was assessed, and this in turn provided the basis for an army where the wealthy were bound to serve and to provide their own military equipment. Those obliged to serve armed as hoplites were said to be part of the *classis*; and those who were not sufficiently wealthy (perhaps the majority) were termed *infra classem* and may have served only as light armed troops (*see* Aulus Gellius, and Festus). That the *classis* was indeed a hoplite formation is confirmed by Festus who comments that

an army, known in his day as an *exercitus*, had i ancient times been called *classis clipeata* (i.e. th *classis* armed with the hoplite shield, *clipeus* being th Latin term for the hoplite shield).

A number of indications make it clear that th Servian political assembly, based on the divisio *classis: infra classem*, arose from a military reform. I later times the developed form of the citizen assen bly still met outside the *pomerium* (the sacred bounc ary of the city of Rome) on the Campus Martius (field dedicated to Mars, the Roman god of war); could only be convened by a magistrate holdin *imperium* (the authority required for military con mand); it was summoned by a trumpet blast (*classicu canere*) with red flags flying on the Janiculum and th Arx when assembled; and the formulae used t summon it included phrases like *exercitum impera* (to command the army) and *exercitum urbanu convocare* (to summon the urban army). The inclu sion of centuries of engineers and musicians als leads to the same conclusion. The fact that th 'Servian' system was entirely unsuitable for recrui ment of a manipular army confirms its predom nantly hoplite character, and it is hardly surprisin that in creating this system Servius Tullius i thought to have introduced hoplite tactics to Rome.

Livy's account of the reforms

Anyone who reads the full historical accounts of earl Rome written by Livy and Dionysius will note tha they describe the 'Servian' reform somewhat diffe ently from the simple division *classis: infra classer* outlined above. Livy's account (1.42.5–43.8) runs a follows:

'The population was divided into classes an centuries and the following arrangement, suitable fo both peace and war, was made based upon the cen sus. 1) Of those who had a census rating of 100,00 *asses* or more he made 80 centuries, 40 of seniors an 40 of juniors, all of whom were called the first Clas The seniors were to be ready to guard the city, an the juniors to wage war abroad. The armour whic these had to provide consisted of helmet, roun shield, greaves, and breast-plate (all of these item made of bronze), to protect the body; their offensiv weapons were the spear and the sword. To this clas were added two centuries of engineers who serve without arms and whose duty was to construct sieg gines in time of war. 2) The Second Class was drawn from those assessed between 75,000 and 00,000 *asses*, and from these 20 centuries (juniors nd seniors) were formed. Their prescribed armour as the same as the first Class except for the breast-late and the rectangular shield in place of the round ne. 3) He determined that the census rating of the hird class should be 50,000 *asses*; the same number f centuries was made and the same arrangement by ges; nor was there any change in their arms except hat greaves were omitted. 4) In the Fourth Class the ensus rating was 25,000 *asses*; the same number of enturies were formed but their equipment was hanged: nothing was given them but a spear and a avelin. 5) The fifth Class was made larger with 30 enturies, and these carried slings with stones for nissiles. Among this class were also the horn-blow-rs and trumpeters who were placed in two centuries. his class was assessed at 11,000 *asses*. 6) The lesser ensus rating contained all the rest of the population, nd of these one century was formed which was xempt from military service.'

This account in Livy is largely paralleled in the escription given by Dionysius in his *Roman Antiqui-es* (4.16.1–18.2). In Dionysius, however, the fourth lass is equipped with shields, swords and spears

where Livy gives just spears and javelins; and the fifth class are given javelins in addition to the slings in Livy. Dionysius adds the two centuries of artisans to the second class, not to the first class as in Livy, and he adds the centuries of musicians to the fourth class rather than to the fifth class. Finally he gives the census rating of the fifth class as a minimum of 12½ *minae* (=12,500 *asses*) rather than 11,000 *asses* as in Livy. These are all minor differences, however, and in every other respect Dionysius' account is remark-ably close to that in Livy.

The descriptions of the Servian army in Dionysius and Livy clearly assume that each of the census classes formed a line in the military forma-tion. Thus the hoplites constituted the first line with

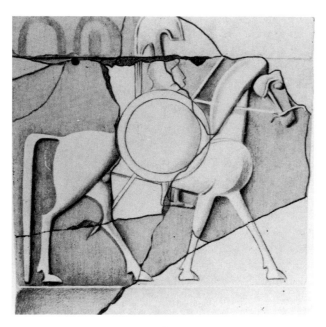

These moulded representations of mounted hoplites from Roman temples are likewise hardly evidence for the adoption of hoplite tactics by the Roman army, rather than simply hoplite equipment.

Furthermore, many moulds used in Rome were also used in other towns in Latium and southern Etruria. Consequently we have no idea whether these moulds were even manufactured in Rome.

the second, third and fourth classes drawn up behind in that order, each with lighter equipment than the previous line. Finally the fifth class acted as skirmishers outside the line of battle. Such a formation contradicts our own description of the Servian army given above, an army composed entirely of hoplites all from a single *classis* supported perhaps by light armed from the *infra classem*. In this case we must examine the descriptions in Dionysius and Livy more closely and show why the five line multi-equipped army cannot truly represent conditions in sixth century BC Rome.

The Servian 40 century legion

This legion, drawn from an assembly with three distinctions of wealth, is itself a development from the original legion which, as we have seen, had only one census class. It is therefore most likely that in its earliest form the 'Servian' army consisted of just one class of hoplites and that classes II to V did not exist. The original Roman phalanx therefore consisted of one *classis* of 40 centuries of 'juniors' (i.e. 4,000 men) equipped in full hoplite panoply with light armed troops drawn from the *infra classem* who were not as yet organized into classes. At some point a further 20 centuries were added (i.e. classes II and III) to make the total 60 centuries. As the army organization expanded with the addition of the extra census classes, the original *classis* of forty centuries was preserved as the first class in the descriptions by Livy and Dionysius.

Fragments of a fictile plaque from the temple of Mater Matuta in Satricum, a town in Latium, showing an armoured warrior carrying a shield with a centaur blazon. Note the triangular plate to defend the groin suspended underneath the tunic. The sculpture dates to the late sixth or early fifth century (Photo: Museo Nazionale di Villa Giulia, Rome)

The 60 century legion

What then is the correct chronology of the development from a legion drawn from a single hoplite class of 40 centuries to one of 60 centuries from an assembly divided into three census classes? Though we can offer no conclusive proof, the most appropriate time for this expansion seems to be the end of the fifth century BC. This was the time when Rome embarked on a ten year war with Veii (traditionally 406–396) which, when placed alongside the commitments generated by membership of the Latin League, must have greatly stretched her military resources. It was then that military pay was introduced for the first time (Livy), a development which looks very much like a measure intended to ease the burden on less wealthy citizens newly brought into the army.

The above analysis has attempted to outline what seems to be the most likely form of the 'Servian

Fragment from the central acroterium of the Sassi Caduti temple at Falerii Veteres, showing an armoured warrior with a curved sabre. The use of auxiliary thigh and arm protectors died out in Greece in the sixth century, but they continued to be popular in Etruria. The sculpture dates to the beginning of the fifth century. (Photo: Museo Nazionale di Villa Giulia, Rome)

...my up to the end of the fifth century BC. Given that ...e primary evidence is so scarce and so difficult to ...terpret, it is hardly surprising that other authors ...ve adopted different approaches. We shall there-...re also discuss alternative views.

Tradition assigns the adoption of hoplite tactics ... the mid sixth-century BC, but there have been ...tempts to down-date the change to the mid-fifth ...ntury. M.P. Nilsson in particular argued that the ...oplite reform occurred with the creation of the first ...ilitary tribunes with consular power (444) and the ...eation of the censorship (443), but few historians ...ow accept the link between the new offices and the ...nsus reform. A strong obstacle to Nilsson's view is ...e fact that the political assembly based on the ...ervian' reform was already in existence *circa* 450 BC ...nd this implies an even earlier date for the army ...form itself. Furthermore, it is very difficult to ...xplain Rome's ability to hold her own in a world ...ominated by Etruscan military power and even to ...rve for herself a significant hegemony in Latium if ...e had not adopted the most advanced military ...ractices of the day. It seems an inescapable conclu-...on therefore that Rome did not lag far behind in ...opying her neighbours.

...ifth century terracotta ...rom Veii showing Aeneas ...arrying Anchises. This ...erracotta is of principal ...nterest as early ...rchaeological evidence ...or the legend of the ...rojan migration to ...atium. It is also of ...nterest as one of the ...arliest representations ...rom Latium of a warrior ...earing a short tunic and ...quipped with greaves, a ...nuscle-cuirass and a ...rested Italo-Attic helmet. ...his combination ...ecomes almost standard ...or all Latin hoplites. ...Photo: Museo Nazionale ...i Villa Giulia, Rome, Inv. ...o. 40272)

Nilsson did, however, draw attention to one piece of evidence for the use of hoplite tactics. This is the incident recorded under 432 BC when the dictator Aulus Postumius had his son executed for leaping out of the battle-line to engage the enemy single handed. A similar event is recorded under 340 BC when the consul T. Manlius Torquatus was said to have executed his son for the same offence (both in Livy). No wonder that elsewhere in Livy's narrative individuals are especially concerned to get permission before engaging in single combat! Whether these reports are genuine is debatable, especially as far as the accuracy of the dates is concerned, but they may conceivably be recollections of the sort of military discipline especially appropriate to the phalanx. We should note, however, that these reports do not help us date the introduction of the phalanx – hoplite warfare could have had a long history even in 432 BC and our mid sixth century BC date must stand. (On this phenomenon see S.P. Oakley, 'Single Combat in the Roman Republic', *Classical Quarterly* 35 (1985) 392–410.)

We have argued above that the hoplite army created by Servius Tullius had a strength of 4,000 and was later augmented to 6,000 at the end of the fifth century BC. Others (though far from all) have suggested that the 60 century army was itself the direct result of Servius' reform and not a later development. That the original Servian army had 60 centuries seems unacceptable because it rejects the relevance of the distinction *classis: infra classem* in favour of less satisfactory evidence. The evidence for the 60 century army is merely that in the descriptions given by Livy and Dionysius the equipment assigned to the first three classes (i.e. the first 60 centuries of 'juniors') belongs to various forms of heavy infantry while that given to classes IV and V is much lighter. But along with many other modern historians the present writers believe that the descriptions in Dionysius and Livy are not based on genuine knowledge of archaic conditions, but are the result of quite arbitrary antiquarian reconstruction, and cannot therefore be pressed as evidence. Furthermore, the assignment of light equipment to the centuries of classes IV and V is bogus because we have no genuine evidence for the light armed ever being organized into centuries (this was certainly not the case in the manipular army).

A more acceptable variant on this interpretation is that, although the army instituted by Servius consisted of 40 centuries, it expanded quickly to a total of 60 centuries by the beginning of the Republic (trad. 509 BC). The difference with the present interpretation is one merely of timing. We prefer to think that the expansion better fits conditions *c.* 400 BC. Those who pursue the theory of an earlier expansion argue that at the beginning of the republic the army was split into two legions, one for each of the two consuls. This is of course possible, but we should note that there is no positive evidence for this and that the proposition relies entirely on intuition. We shall discuss the question of the increase in the number of legions in further detail below.

Our conclusion from all this has three parts. Hoplite tactics were introduced into Rome, via Etruria, in the mid sixth century BC. The earliest Roman hoplite army was composed of 40 centuries of hoplites. At some point before the creation of an additional legion the 40 centuries were augmented by the addition of a further 20 centuries. Some suggest that this took place before the collapse of the Roman monarchy (trad. 509 BC) but the present authors prefer *c.* 400 BC as a more likely date.

Italian muscle-cuirass. This example, in the British Museum, is from Ruvo in South Italy and dates to the second half of the fourth century. Italian muscle-cuirasses can be easily distinguished from Greek examples as they have no shoulder-guards. (Photo: N.V. Sekunda)

EARLY CAVALRY

The sex suffragia

It should come as no surprise that, just as with the centuries of infantry, the Servian cavalry organization described by Livy and Dionysius is not genuinely archaic. Livy describes how Servius added twelve centuries to the pre-existing cavalry force of six centuries:

'So with the infantry force armed and organized in this way, 12 centuries of cavalry were enrolled from among the leading men of the state. He formed a further six centuries (three had been created by Romulus) with the same traditional names. For the purchase of horses 10,000 *asses* were given from the state treasury, and for their upkeep rich widows were assigned to pay 2,000 *asses* each year.'

The six centuries to which Servius is supposed to have added his twelve were titled Tities *priores* and *posteriores*, Ramnes *priores* and *posteriores*, and Luceres *priores* and *posteriores*. In later times these six centuries had a special status and were known as the *sex suffragia* ('the six votes'), a title which distinguished them from the remaining twelve equestrian centuries in the *comitia centuriata* (Livy, Cicero, Festus 452L). It is almost certain therefore that there had once been only six centuries of *equites* and that the addition of a further twelve could not have been the work of Servius Tullius. The error made by Roman historians was to assume that the final total of 1,800 *equites* in the late republic was not the product of a later increase in their numbers (for which see below) but had been instituted at the very beginning by Servius. Furthermore, they did not realize that 1,800 is an impossibly high figure for the cavalry resources of archaic Rome.

It would seem superficially obvious that the *sex suffragia* of *equites* reflects an original force of 600 cavalry, but a significant problem here is that we have no evidence of cavalry in later times being organized into centuries as was the infantry. Later Roman cavalry were organized into *turmae* of 30 men, each ivided into three *decuriae* of ten men. Indeed the ncient religious ceremony known as the *transvectio quitum*, which was probably instituted in the early fth century BC, was performed by six *turmae* and ot six centuries.

The retention of the titles Tities, Ramnes and uceres suggests that the Servian reform itself did ot fundamentally alter the organization or recruitnent of the Roman *equites*. They remained drawn rom the three tribes and there seems to have been no pecial census rating for service as an *eques* over and bove that of the infantry. Livy states merely that ney were drawn from the 'leading men of the state' *x primioribus civitatis*).

These considerations combine to suggest that he *sex suffragia* were not six centuries of true cavalry. t seems that the three tribal centuries of *equites* urvived the Servian reform as an élite hoplite band, ot as true cavalry, and assumed the honorific title of enturies *priores*. The date and circumstances of the ddition of the three centuries of Tities, Ramnes and uceres *posteriores* are quite obscure. Perhaps an xpansion in the 'leading men of the state' dictated an xpansion in the number of equestrian centuries. Vhether this occurred at the time of the Servian eform or at a later date is uncertain.

The designations *priores* and *posteriores* suggest ot only a notional position in the battle-line. Greek avalrymen would be individually attended by nounted grooms who would withdraw behind the avalry when the troops were formed up. Perhaps the *quites posteriores* fulfilled a theoretical relationship of ;rooms to the *equites priores*; and it may be that this notional doubling suggested to the antiquarians that t some stage the *priores* had made use of two horses. nteresting details have been preserved by Granius Licinianus and Festus concerning the supply of two norses to some of the cavalry: 'The Romans used the ame number of horses, that is two, in battle so that they might transfer to a fresh one when the other was worn out; the double amount given to the cavalrymen for two horses was called the *aes pararium*' (Festus); 'I shall not pass over the cavalry which Tarquin introduced in such a way that the centuries of *priores* led two horses into battle' (Granius Licinianus).

The public horse and true cavalry

The first plausible evidence for the establishment of a force of true cavalry at Rome comes in 403 BC: during the final and decisive struggle with Veii. As has already been noted, this war saw the introduction of military pay and probably also the expansion of the infantry Legion. Livy records that 403 was the first year in which cavalrymen served on their own horses and that they were then rewarded by the introduction of pay for the cavalry. Such volunteers serving on their own mounts were called *equites equo privato* or *equites suis merentes*.

How funds were raised to provide this pay is unknown. In the later Republic Rome also main-

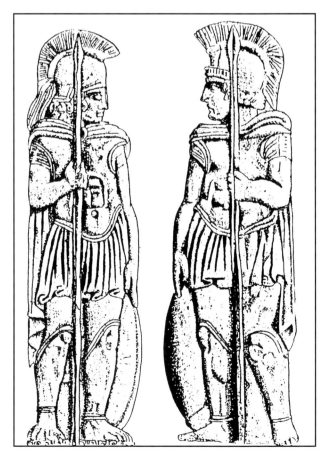

These two bone plaques from Palestrina, dating to the fourth century, belong to a series of laminae of different sizes, which probably once formed the veneer of a magistrate's seat of office (sella curulis). This pair of hoplite warriors wear the dress and equipment typical of Latin hoplites of the period: crested Italo-Attic helmets, muscle-cuirasses, and greaves, together with a short tunic and cloak. Note the round clasps securing the cloak. (Photo: Museo Nazionale di Villa Giulia, Rome, Inv. nos. 13236, 13237. Courtesy Montvert Publications)

Front and back views of the handle of a lid of a Praenestine cist showing two warriors carrying the body of a third home. This cista is one of the earlier ones in the series and probably dates to the end of the fourth century. Unlike the overwhelming majority of depictions of hoplites from Latium they do not wear greaves, and they wear the composite cuirass instead of the muscle-cuirass. The muscle-cuirass may not have been universal in Latium at this period, or perhaps Etruscan hoplites are meant to be shown. (Photo: Museo Nazionale di Villa Giulia, Rome, Inv. 25210)

tained another force of cavalry whose mounts were provided at public expense, and who were paid an allowance for fodder. These cavalry were called *equites equo publico*. It is not known whether the institution of *equites equo publico* existed before the establishment of the *equites equo privato* in 406 BC, but this seems highly unlikely as raising the resources to supply horses and fodder required much more strenuous fiscal effort than simply providing cavalry pay. Consequently we are drawn to the conclusion that prior to 406 BC the title *eques* was purely honorific.

In contemporary Sparta and Corinth the provision of horses for the cavalry was a fiscal requirement imposed on the estates of widows and orphans, which were administered by the state upon the death of the head of a household. Livy records the imposition by Servius of taxes on orphans and widows, but the *aes equestre* (the tax to provide horses) and the *aes hordearium* (the tax to provide fodder) were probably later developments which have been incorrectly attributed to Servius. In a different strand of the Roman historical tradition to that in Livy, we find the introduction of similar taxes attributed to M. Furius Camillus in 403, this time on unmarried men and orphans (Plutarch and Valerius Maximus). It is possible therefore that the institution of *equites equo publico* was established then.

We presume that the original *equites equo privato* were by and large recruited from the 'leading citizens' of the *sex suffragia* (by this time a political grouping rather than a military organisation), and the establishment of the *equites equo publico* enabled a 600 to serve as cavalry. The expansion of the *equites equo publico* to a strength of 1,800 probably only occurred towards the end of the fourth century BC (*see* below). In the Second Punic War, when the number of *equites equo publico* was insufficient to provide the cavalry complement of a vastly increased number of legions, the institution of *equites equo privato* had to be relied on once again.

As has already been mentioned, tradition maintained that before the Servian Reform three tribal centuries of *equites* had existed, but it is doubtful whether these 'horsemen' ever operated as true cavalry on the hoplite battlefield. In Archaic Greece forces of true cavalry were only maintained by Thessaly and Boeotia. In these two states there existed an aristocracy sufficiently wealthy and

owerful to provide their own cavalry horses. Else-
here Athens had created a force of 300 cavalry by
57, later expanded to 1,200 *circa* 443; Sparta created
force of 400 cavalry in 424, and few other Greek
ates had any force of cavalry worth mentioning
efore the closing decades of the fifth century BC.

The principal reason for the late emergence of
ivalry in Greece was the difficulty in providing
orses, or compensation for privately owned horses
lled in battle, and allowances for fodder. Before the
ivention of the horse collar in the medieval period
cen were used to plough and to pull carts, and the
orse was simply used as an extravagant means of
ansport. Aristocrats with the wealth to maintain
orses were few and were reluctant to gamble their
xpensive pets on the battlefield. Like the hoplite
ity-states of Greece, the hoplite city-states of Italy
eeded to develop methods of raising state revenues
efore they could subsidize and compensate horse-
wning aristocrats for their service as cavalrymen.
onsequently it is unlikely that Rome possessed any
ue force of cavalry before the last decades of the
fth century BC.

THE EXPANSION OF ROMAN MILITARY STRENGTH

By the end of the fourth century BC the Roman army
definitely comprised four legions. Unfortunately
there is no specific ancient testimony telling us exactly when and how new legions came into being.
Instead we have to proceed using a mixture of guess-
work, assessment of probabilities, and inference. The
type of problem confronting us should be clear when
we recognize that an increase in the number of
Roman legions could be the result of two quite
different processes. On the one hand, existing manpower could have been split into a larger number of
units (i.e. a purely organizational development in-
volving no increase in manpower). On the other it
could be the case that new units were created by
means of increased conscription. It is quite possible,
moreover, that both processes operated at different
stages of development. What follows is an outline of
the most likely pattern of development in the fourth
century BC.

The infantry

We have already attempted to show that the Roman
army *c.* 400 consisted of a single legion of 6,000 men.
In 366, however, after many years of electing military
tribunes with consular power as the main officers of
state, Rome resumed the election of just two annual
consuls. It is likely that it was as a response to this
that the legion was split into two. At this time Rome
cannot have been in a position to recruit extra troops
from thin air; manpower must therefore have remained the same and was now divided into two

Scene from the painted frescoes of the François Tomb from Vulci. Dating from the second half of the fourth century, the tomb shows both mythological and historical scenes. In this historical scene the Etruscan Aule Vipinas (Latin Aulus Vibenna) kills one Venthi Cau[ ]plsachs,
possibly a Faliscan rather than a Roman, but a Latin for sure. He is equipped with hoplite shield, muscle-cuirass and greaves, and dressed in the short tunic we have seen to be typical of Latin hoplites at this period. The tunic colour is red.

This Praenestine cist has not been firmly dated yet, but the equipment shown indicates a date on the eve of the adoption of manipular weapons and tactics in Latium. The traditional hoplite shield and spear, the muscle-cuirass, greaves, tunic and cloak are retained unchanged, but the Italo-Attic helmet has been replaced with helmets of the Montefortino type. (Photo: Hermitage, St Petersburg, Inv. B 619)

legions each of 3,000 men. We know from Livy, however, that by 311 Rome had four legions. He comments that this year saw 'the election by the people of sixteen military tribunes for distribution amongst the four legions, whereas these had previously been almost exclusively in the gift of the dictators and consuls' and the implication is that the existence of four legions was a recent development. These legions were undoubtedly formations organized around the maniple and, if we follow Polybius' description of the manipular legion, consisted of 3,000 heavy infantry and 1,200 light-armed. The total force was therefore 12,000 heavy infantry and 4,800 light troops: more than double that available in 366.

Such a large increase becomes understandable when we consider Rome's successes in the fourth century BC, particularly her defeat of the Latins and the conditions of the peace made in 338. Rome imposed terms on her defeated enemies which significantly increased the pool of citizen manpower. Not only were the towns of Lanuvium, Aricia, Nomentum, Pedum, Velitrae and Antium all given full Roman citizenship; but a new type of citizenship was also introduced. This was the *civitas sine suffragio* (citizenship without the vote), a status whereby the holder was liable for taxation and military service but could not participate in Roman political assemblies or hold office. This *civitas sine suffragio* was given to the important Campanian towns of Capua, Suessula and Cumae (plus Acerrae in 332), and the Volscian towns of Fundi and Formiae (and Privernum in 329).

These grants in themselves hugely increased available manpower, but Rome pursued another policy which must also have had the same effect. This was the appropriation of some of the land of a number of defeated opponents. Land confiscation allowed the settlement of Roman citizens – citizens who previously may have been too poor to be liable to military service under the 'Servian' system. But now, with their new land, they would become sufficiently wealthy to qualify for military service.

Thus even without the creation of *civitas sine suffragio* Rome would probably have increased her available manpower. But with all these measures combined, the increase must have been colossal. The census records for the fourth century BC are generally considered to be very unreliable, and we are therefore unable to quantify this increase precisely, but we can at least note that because of the expansion of the mid fourth century BC the area of land occupied by Roman citizens increased from *circa* 1,500 square kilometres to *circa* 5,500. And we should not forget that allied communities possessing treaties with Rome also had to supply their own contingents for Rome's wars.

It should therefore cause us no surprise that sometime between 338 and 311 Rome was able to double her infantry force to four legions.

Legionary blazons

From the evidence given above it seems that at some date after 338 BC the Roman army comprised four legions, and for a number of years before manipular equipment and tactics were introduced these legions may have been equipped as hoplites. Pliny, after telling us that Marius gave the Roman legions their eagle standards during his second consulship in 104 BC, mentions that previously the legions carried eagle standards as their first badge, but that in addition they carried four others; wolves, minotaurs, horses and boars going in front of the various *ordines*. *Ordo* usually means 'rank' and so the natural interpretation of Pliny's words would be that these standards would e carried in front of the various ranks of the manipular army: that is the *triarii, principes* and *hastati*. There is an obvious problem that four standards do not go into three ranks, so it seems reasonable to assume that Pliny has misunderstood his source, presumably one of the 'antiquarians'. Given that there were traditionally four legions from the closing decades of the fourth century onwards, it is tempting to assume that Pliny's source was describing the four legionary standards.

Two of the four legions would have been the two Roman legions most probably formed after the legionary split in 366 BC. For these two 'Roman' legions the devices of the wolf and the boar would be the most appropriate symbols. The wolf, together with the woodpecker, was the animal sacred to Mars (Plutarch, *Life of Romulus* 4). We have already met the she-wolf, sacred to Mars, in the legend of Romulus and Remus, which was already reaching its finished form during the fourth century. The wolf does not appear by itself as a symbol in Roman republican coinage, but the she-wolf suckling Romulus and Remus does, and it is tempting to assume that this is the symbol (perhaps of *Legio I*)

Following the extension of citizenship to the Campanians, the human-faced bull starts to appear on Roman coins. This half or quarter litra, showing the protome of a human-headed bull on its reverse, was issued c. 300 BC. (Photo: Hirmer Fotoarchiv, München)

which Pliny's source is describing. The significance of the boar is less certain. We might note that in Imperial times the boar was one of the symbols of the *Legio X Fretensis* and the symbol of the *Legio XX Valeria Victrix*. Its significance has not been explained so far, but it was perhaps originally the symbol of Quirinus, the Sabine equivalent of Mars, who had continued to have a separate cult existence in Rome after the amalgamation of the two founding communities around 600 BC.

The symbols of horse and minotaur are even more difficult to explain. However, they may allude to the origins of the two new legions. In Greek iconography the minotaur is shown as a bull-headed human, and, indeed, such a beast is shown on an early moulded relief from Rome. The human-headed bull is, however, much more common, especially on Sicilian and Italian coins, where it is usually interpreted as representing some or other river-god. The human-headed bull was also the symbol of the Campanians. This is presumably the minotaur referred to by Pliny's source. Thus it may be suggested

Coin struck in Neapolis by the Campanian League circa 340 BC, bearing the device of a human-faced bull, presumably the badge of the Campanian people as a whole. The same device occurs on coins of other Campanian cities, such as Cales and Hyria, as well as on coins of Rome itself.

that one of the four legions of the late fourth century was formed from Campanians to whom Roman citizenship had been extended, hence they took as their badge the former national symbol of Campania.

The horse cannot be explained in a similar way, as it appears on Italian coins issued by a large number of towns. Thus it cannot be isolated as the symbol of a particular region. We note, however, that citizenship was extended to both Latin and Volscian communities at about the same time as it was to the Campanians, and it may be that these communities made up the fourth legion. On Roman republican coins the horse frequently appears as a device on those which bear the head of Mars on the obverse.

The cavalry

We have already suggested that the Roman army of the very late fifth century BC had a maximum of six centuries of cavalry, and that these were represented in the electoral assembly by the *sex suffragia*. We have also seen that the further twelve centuries of the electoral assembly which brought the total up to eighteen were a later addition. It is interesting therefore that the twelve additional centuries amount to the total cavalry component of a four legion manipular army (*see* Polybius). It seems very likely therefore that the introduction of the four legion army was accompanied by an overhaul of the cavalry in which 1,200 new *equites equo publico* were created, 300 per legion. The existing force represented in the *sex suffragia* must have been relegated to a ceremonial and electoral role only. A hint of this large increase in cavalry resources can be found in the *Ineditum Vaticanum* whose author stressed Rome's need greatly to augment her cavalry forces in order to face the Samnites (quoted below).

Etruscan Mirror, dating to the late fourth century or early third century. In Etruscan iconology, influenced by the struggle against Roman expansion, it is normal for Etruscans to be represented as Greeks and Romans as Trojans. This arose out of the commonly held belief that the Roman nation grew from Trojan immigrants originally settled in Latium by Aeneas. By extension it could be argued that on this mirror Hercules (Herkle) represents an Etruscan while the Amazon Hephleta represents a Roman. As a shield blazon Hephleta has the head of a human-headed bull: perhaps a Roman legionary shield blazon. The martial goddess Minerva looks on.

The Earliest Roman Warriors,
c.700 BC
1: 'Romulus'
2: 'Remus'

A

B

Horatius at the Bridge, 508 BC
1: Etruscan Hoplite
2: Roman Hoplite
3: Latin Hoplite

C

The Venetic Fighting System, fifth century BC
1: Pikeman
2: Shield-bearer
3: Hoplite
4: Axe-man

D

Roman Hoplites defeated by Celts, fourth century BC
1, 2, 3: Roman Hoplites
4: Celtic horseman
5: Celtic swordsman

E

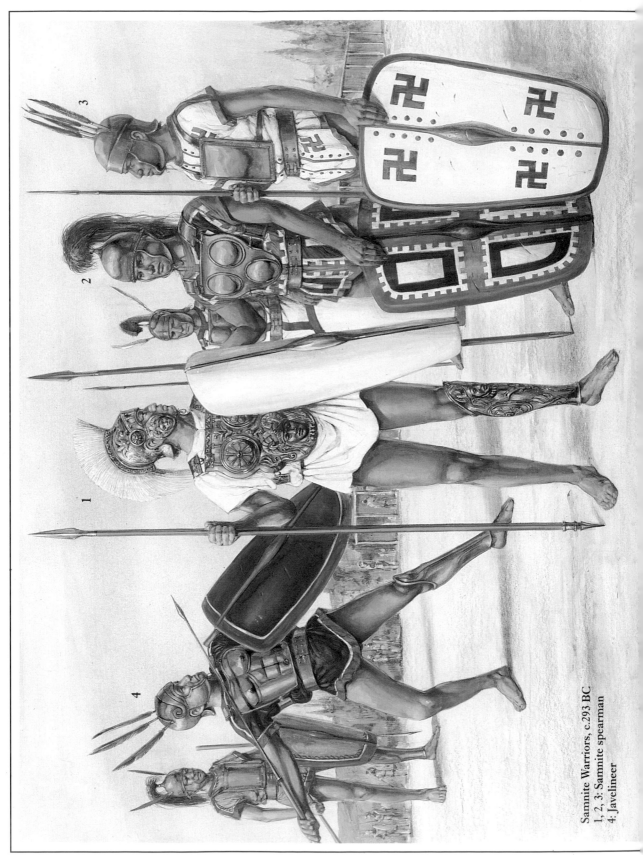

Samnite Warriors, c.293 BC
1, 2, 3: Samnite spearman
4: Javelineer

F

Sacrifice establishing a treaty between Romans and Samnites
1: Roman Lituus-bearer   3: Roman General
2: Samnite General   4: Priests

G

Roman Hastati fight one
of Pyrrhus' elephants
1: Roman Hastati
2: Epirote war elephant

The expansion of the strength of the *equites equo publico* to 1,800 seems not to have been the only increase in Roman cavalry resources. In 340 1,600 Capuan *equites* were granted Roman citizenship for their loyalty to Rome at a time when the rest of Capua had deserted to Rome's enemies. In addition the Capuans were forced to provide each cavalryman with 450 *denarii* to pay for the upkeep of their horses (Livy).

MANIPULAR WARFARE

Whilst hoplite warfare remained dominant from the middle of the sixth century BC down through the fourth in Latium and many areas of Italy, elsewhere in the peninsula other forms of warfare were ascendant. Eventually one of these, manipular warfare, was adopted by the Roman legions. legions. Essentially the manipular formation consisted of a number of lines of infantry, each line consisting of blocks of troops (maniples) with wide spaces separating the maniples, enabling them to advance or withdraw independently of the movement of the battle-line as a whole. Each line of maniples might be equipped differently.

At some point during the fourth century BC the Roman hoplite phalanx was abandoned and replaced by the much more flexible 'manipular' formation. When and why this took place are obvious questions, but they are not so easily answered.

The Gallic invasions

Many have stressed the importance of the defeat at the Allia at the hands of the Gauls, and have claimed that this disaster led the Romans to adopt the manipular formation. Dionysius and Plutarch certainly believed that some form of tactical change was employed when the Gauls next returned. Both claim that it was under the guidance of M. Furius Camillus that the Romans adopted the oval shield (*scutum*) and the heavy javelin (*pilum*) to replace the round shield (*clipeus*) and the thrusting spear (*hasta*) of the hoplites. Neither author explicitly records the introduction of maniples, but this must be assumed since the adoption of these weapons without the appropriate manipular formation would be a nonsense.

Dionysius tells how the Roman soldiers ducked down under the blows of the Gallic swords and took them on the shield, while striking at the enemies' groin with the sword. Plutarch gives a slightly different variation, saying oddly that the Gallic blows were taken on the *pilum*, but we should treat such descriptions with great caution. We know, for instance, that a different sort of tactic had been employed much later in defeating the Gauls at Telamon in 225 BC. Here the first Roman line was equipped with the *hasta* instead of the *pilum* and the *hastae* were used to take the initial blows of the enemy. It seems difficult therefore to believe that earlier Romans, as according to Plutarch at least, had defeated the Gauls by doing precisely the opposite and abandoning the *hasta*. What seems to have happened is that these late authors knew that the Gauls had been defeated and

European shields of the Late Bronze Age and early Iron Age frequently have either 'U-notch' or 'V-notch' decoration. Such shields are called Herzsprung shields after the site where the principal shield in the series was found. This example of a 'U-notch' shield from Bohemia is closest to the shields shown on the Certosa situla, even though it is much earlier in date. (Photo: J. Coles)

Reconstruction of the Certosa Situla. The uppermost register shows the four groups of

Infantrymen discussed in the text. (after P. Ducati, La Situla della Certosa, 1923)

assumed that some tactical innovation must have been employed. With this in mind they gave a garbled and unlikely version (for which they probably had no direct evidence) of later tactics.

There is a further and a stronger argument against the Gauls acting as the catalyst for the introduction of manipular tactics and equipment at Rome. The Romans will presumably have copied manipular tactics from an enemy who had shown this formation to be superior to the phalanx. This enemy could hardly have been the Gauls since they certainly did not use manipular tactics. The origins of manipular warfare are obscure, and the existing literary fragments shed no light on the question. The earliest possible depiction of manipular warfare comes on an object known as the Certosa Situla.

The Certosa Situla

The situla is decorated with four registers showing an animal scene, a banqueting scene, a sacrificial procession and a parade of warriors. It is the parade with which we are principally concerned. The parade opens with two cavalrymen dressed in a fringed tunic, covered by what appears to be some kind of cuirass made out of coarsely-woven thick textile material, and pot helmet. They carry palstave ax over the shoulder. It is possible that the two hors men represent an illustrative attempt to indicate th the infantry line was supported by cavalry statione on either flank. The horsemen are then followed b one group of five infantrymen, and then by thr other groups of four. The warriors of each group a identically equipped, but each group is different.

The first group of warriors carry long ov shields. The shields have a narrow border and in th centre a boss of 'Herzsprung' shape. The fringe hem of a tunic is shown beneath the shield on some the figures, and it is possible that a textile cuiras similar to that worn by the horsemen, would ha been worn behind the shield. The spear is conside ably longer than those carried by the other figures the situla, and it ends in a long butt-spike. Th warriors wear a 'disk and stud' helmet. The helmet held on by a strap passing under the chin. Whe these and other figures from the Certosa Situla a illustrated, the photographs show the cheeks of the warriors represented by bulges punched out of th bronze sheeting. These should not be interpreted metal disks attached to the chin strap.

The second group of infantrymen carry squa shields with rounded edges and a square boss at th centre. The third group of warriors carry rou shields with rims decorated with a triangular patter As the shields of both these groups of warriors rea most to the knee, we are unable to see whether they wear tunics or any body armour. Both groups wear pot helmets and carry hoplite spears with quite wide leaf-shaped points. All three groups of spearmen carry their spears reversed, with the points towards the ground. This may represent standard battlefield practice during the advance, or it could have funerary significance.

It could be suggested that these groups of spearmen are intended to represent a manipular battle-line in two dimensions, and are thus ancestors of the Roman *acies triplex* of *hastati*, *principes* and *triarii*. Unlike the Roman battle-line, however, the Venetic warriors all carry fighting spears rather than javelins. Other examples of Veneto-Illyrian bronze work, such as the Arnoaldi situla, show warriors

with oblong shields, helmets and a pair of javelins, and the Carpena decorated plaque shows warriors with round shields, helmets and a pair of javelins. Such troops would use armament much more appropriate for precursors of Roman *manipularii*, and it may be, indeed, that this type of weaponry gradually replaced that shown on the Certosa Situla.

Behind the three groups of spearmen march a final group of four unshielded infantrymen, wearing fringed tunics, textile cuirasses like those worn by the cavalrymen and conical helmets and carrying palstave axes over their shoulders. What are these figures supposed to represent? In the Roman manipular battle line the light infantry commenced the fight by engaging the enemy with javelins before the two battle-lines closed. When this happened the light infantry withdrew through the gaps between the maniples and re-formed behind the third line. These Venetic axe men may also be light infantry. On the other hand the battlefield role of the axemen may have been to finish off enemy wounded as the triple battle-line advanced. Conical helmets of similar type are also shown on other pieces of bronze-work produced by the Veneto-Illyrian culture.

Whatever the validity of these varied speculations may be in detail, it certainly does seem that in the Certosa Situla we can see a representation of a precursor of the manipular tactics which would even-

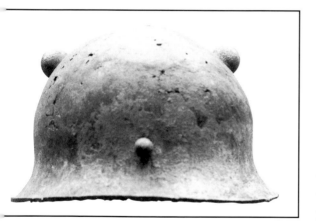

Above: Bronze Italian pot-helmet, once crested, found near Ancona in the Picenum and now in the British Museum. These pot-helmets remained popular within the Picene and adjacent regions much later than in other areas of Italy. The resemblance between this helmet and those shown on the Certosa Situla is obvious. (Photo: N.V. Sekunda)

This example of a 'Disc and stud' helmet is similar to those worn by the first group of warriors on the Certosa Situla. It is from Slovenia, within the Venetic-Illyrian cultural region. (Photo: Narodni Muzej, Ljubljana)

tually spread to Rome at the end of the fourth century BC. It should be noted, however, that the varied and multiple battle-line which is shown on the Certosa Situla is not repeated on other surviving examples of decorated bronze-work left by the Veneto-Illyrian culture showing military scenes.

Samnite warfare

Since the Gauls did not cause the Romans to change their formation and weapons it is almost certain that the Samnites were responsible. Indeed this was believed by some ancient authors. Athenaeus wrote that 'they learned the use of the *scutum* from the Samnites'; Sallust said that 'our ancestors . . . took their offensive and defensive weapons from the Samnites'; and the author of the *Ineditum Vaticanum* wrote: 'We did not have the traditional Samnite *scutum* nor did we have the *pilum*. But we fought with round shields and spears; nor were we strong in cavalry either but all or the greater part of the Roman army was

infantry. But when we became involved in a war with the Samnites we were equipped with the *scutum* and the *pilum* and had forced ourselves to fight as cavalry so with foreign weapons and copied tactics we enslaved those who had developed a conceited pride in themselves.'

The explanation is clear. In their wars against the Samnites over the rough terrain of central southern Italy the hoplite phalanx proved to be much less effective than the more flexible formation used by the Samnites. The latter employed a large number of smaller and more manoeuvrable units (maniples) of soldiers equipped with heavy javelins and the *scutum*.

Fortunately two passages in Livy contain much valuable information on the dress, equipment and organization of the Samnite army during the last two Samnite Wars. This information is frequently dismissed as extremely untrustworthy by modern historians. In what follows, however, we have assumed that what Livy tells us, although distorted, especially

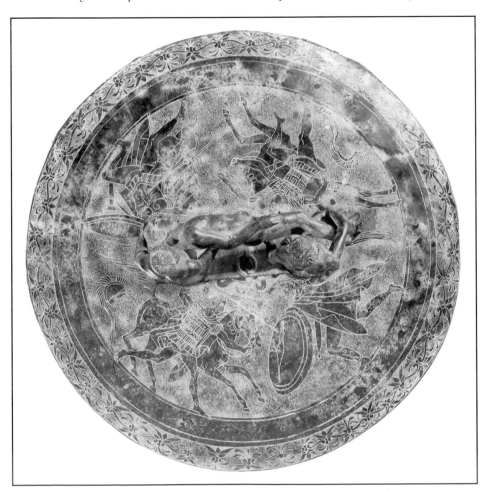

This detailed photograph of a cist from Praeneste now in Berlin presumably shows a Samnite infantryman attacking a dismounted cavalryman, possibly an Etruscan. The Samnite carries a scutum a sword and a javelin, and wears a single greave on his left leg. This representation is highly important in providing archaeological evidence to support the contention of Livy and others that the Samnites fought with a single greave. (Photo: Berlin, Staatliche Museen

in its chronology, is ultimately based on a relatively sound near-contemporary source. This information allows us to reconstruct a quite detailed picture of the Samnite army and perhaps, therefore, sheds some light on the versions of their tactics and equipment adopted by the Romans.

Livy tells us that in 310 the Samnite infantry all carried trapezoidal *scuta* which were wider at the top, in order to protect the breast and shoulders, with a level or flat top (i.e. not curving or oval in shape), but somewhat narrower at the bottom in order to allow better mobility. According to Livy the Samnite warriors wore a 'sponge' (*spongia*) in front of their breast. Clearly what is being described is the characteristic chest-protector (*pectorale*) widely worn during the fourth century, although it is a complete mystery why the word *spongia* is used. The left leg alone was covered with a greave. They wore crested helmets to make them appear taller. Spears are not mentioned, but if these Samnites were fighting in manipular formation the weapon used may have varied from maniple to maniple, some carrying a pair of javelins, others carrying spears.

Livy also tells us that the Samnite infantry was divided into two corps, each of which he calls an *exercitus* (usually translated as 'army'). The first wore tunics of bleached white linen and shields inlaid with silver. The other wore parti-coloured tunics and had shields inlaid with gold. An uncertain restoration in this section of Livy would also give baldrics and sheaths in silver to the first corps and in gold to the second. The first *exercitus* was given the post of honour on the right wing, while the second was drawn up on the left. Livy adds that it was the custom of the Samnites to consecrate themselves before battle, and this is why they dressed themselves in white and whitened their arms, for white was the colour of religious purity.

Further information is added by a second passage in Livy which describes the organization of the Samnite army before the Battle of Aquilonia in 293. A levy was held throughout Samnium, which, when concentrated at Aquilonia, amounted to 40,000 men. All who did not report for duty were to forfeit their life to Jupiter. In the middle of the camp an area some 60 metres (200 feet) in all directions was enclosed with wicker hurdles and was roofed over with linen. Here a sacrifice was made by Ovius Paccius according to ancient rites preserved on linen rolls in his possession. Livy mentions that the Samnite army

This terracotta statuette of Minerva shows the goddess carrying a trapezoidal shield. Such shields existed as gladiatorial weapons, but it would be unusual for the goddess to carry a purely gladiatorial weapon, rather than one also used in war. (Photo: Museo 'Sigismondo Castromediano', Lecce)

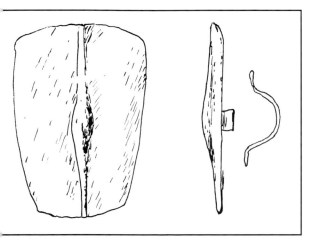

Gladiatorial relief from Venafro, dating from circ 50 BC, now walled in the entrance to the Palazzo Cimorelli. The right half of the lower register show a fight between a 'Julian' Bassus and a 'Cassian' Chrestus. Bassus holds a 'trapezoidal' scutum. (Photo: Istituto Archeologico Germanico, Rome: Neg. Rom 31.3001; 75.2762)

was commanded by an *imperator*, perhaps Ovius Paccius himself. The *imperator* selected ten of the most eminent of the Samnites, and they then chose a further ten, until the number of the chosen band rose to 16,000 in strength. These soldiers then swore a solemn oath over the sacrifices, which were guarded by centurions with drawn swords. These were called the 'Linen Legion' (*legio linteata*) after the linen roof of the enclosure, and they were given splendid arms and crested helmets to distinguish them from the rest. The other *exercitus* comprised 'a little over twenty thousand men'; presumably 24,000 men to conform with the total of 40,000.

Livy gives the impression that the *legio linteata* had just been formed in the camp at Aquilonia in 293, but it is perfectly obvious that he is describing the same sacred band as was in operation in 310. On the eve of the Battle of Aquilonia Livy puts a speech in the mouth of Lucius Papirius, the Roman commander, who tells us that 'long ago' a silver and gilt Samnite army had been destroyed by his father. He seems to be referring to the conflict of 310 some 17 years previously. The whole speech, however, is best

regarded as a rhetorical embellishment by Livy. I the same passage he refers to the Samnite shields a being painted as well as silvered. This perhaps im plies that the shields of the *legio linteata* were painte white, and only the metal components were deco rated in silver. It seems obvious that Livy is manipu lating the primary source which was available to hin and that the *legio linteata* was not a creation made jus for the campaign of 293, but was rather a long standing Samnite military institution. Assuming tha the Romans were able to field a four-legion army c some 16,000 men or thereabouts regularly in the lat fourth century, the Samnites may have felt com pelled to create within their military system an élit force of comparable size, given better training tha the rest of the army, to take the field against th Romans. Thus the *legio linteata* was a military insti tution comparable to the bodies of *epilektoi*, o 'picked' troops, formed by Greek armies, especiall from the 360s onwards; a military institution which had already spread to the Syracusan army o Dionysius I in the early years of the century.

By adding some further details to the informa

This famous pectorale, of the trilobate variety, was found in North Africa, where it had evidently been brought by an Italian mercenary in Carthaginian service. Colour photographs of the cuirass show it to be plated in white metal, either silver or tin, which suggests the possibility that it was an heirloom, and may even originally have been manufactured for use by a member of the legio linteata. A number of the decorative motifs, such as the bucranium fixing the shoulder plate, or the lintel decorated with paterae (flat bowls for sacrificial libations), supported by the columns of a temple colonnade, are concerned with sacrifice and perhaps refer to the sacrifice and oath taken by members of the legio linteata. The principal decorative feature is a head of Minerva wearing a triple-crested helmet, which follows Greek representations of Athena Promachos dating to the late fourth century. (Photo: Musée National de Bardo, Tunis)

ion imparted by Livy in these two passages, we can suggest a possible organizational structure for the *legio linteata*. The total citizen levy of the Samnite people which Livy mentions corresponds to the total citizen body (*touto*) of the Samnites, and the officer whom Livy calls an *imperator* may have been the chief civil and military magistrate of the Samnites, the *meddix tuticus*. Beneath him, the ten officers first elected may have been termed *meddices minores*, each in charge of a force of 1,600 *manipulares*, though we have no idea what these sub-units may have been called. Within his description of the events of 293 BC, Livy mentions 'the linen cohorts', and twenty cohorts of Samnites, each of about 400 men. Samnite cohorts of unspecified size are also mentioned in other passages. Elsewhere Livy mentions eight cohorts of Hernici operating in 362 BC, each numbering 400 men: that is, a total force of 3,200 men, double the size of one sub-unit of the *legio linteata*. Elsewhere in his *Histories* Livy uses terms such as

maniple and cohort quite carelessly and anachronistically, but, given the combined weight of the passages mentioned above, it is difficult to avoid the conclusion that each of the ten divisions of the *legio linteata* numbering 1,600 men were divided into four cohorts of 400. Livy also mentions centurions in his description of the oath-taking, so it would be reasonable further to suggest that each of these cohorts was divided into two maniples and four centuries, each maniple having a *centurio prior* and *posterior* along the lines of later Roman practice.

The other *exercitus*, comprising the remainder of the Samnite infantry, would presumably have been divided along similar lines into 15 units of 1,600 men, each with its cohorts and maniples. If there were only two maniples to the cohort, it would be reasonable to deduce that the Samnite battle-line would have been drawn up into two lines of maniples, an *acies duplex*, with the first line of maniples equipped with javelins (*pila*), and the second line with fighting-spears (*hastae*).

The Manipular army in Livy

Livy (8.8) describes a Roman manipular formation drawn up in five lines. The first is composed of 15 maniples of *hastati* each with an extra 20 light-armed soldiers. The second line also has 15 maniples, this time of *principes*. Behind these stand in sequence the *triarii*, *rorarii*, and *accensi*. Livy gives few details concerning the equipment except that the light-armed *rorarii* and *accensi* have the javelin and spear, while the *triarii* have the *hasta*: all are armed with the *scutum*. We are left to assume that the *hastati* and *principes* were armed with the *pilum*. Nor is his description of tactical deployment complete. Livy speaks of the first three lines engaging the enemy one after the other, but he assigns no specific role to the *rorarii* and *accensi*. Although there is a certain internal logic in Livy's account, which makes a literal interpretation of his manipular system perfectly possible, severe doubts arise concerning the historicity of Livy's description. We know that *rorarii* was an early name for light-armed troops and that *accensi* were non-combatant baggage attendants (Varro). Neither of these pieces of information fits with Livy's description. A recent historian writing on this subject has said: 'This whole farrago appears as an antiquarian reconstruction, concocted out of scat-

Italo-Attic helmets of this type were in widespread use among the Samnites. This fourth century example, now in the British Museum, is said to have come from Vulci. (Photo: N.V. Sekunda)

tered pieces of information and misinformation mostly to do with the manipular army. One of its underlying features seems to be a strained attempt to establish some sort of relation between the new military order and the five categories of the census classification.'

Livy's account must surely be rejected. We should rather assume that the Roman form of the manipular system had just three lines (of *hastati*, *principes* and *triarii*), plus attached light infantry (*rorarii*), from its very beginning. Elsewhere we have also assumed that it had roughly the same complement as the later Republican legion described by Polybius. It seems that Livy is basing his account on a source which describes how the *rorarii* retire behind the *triarii* following the initial phases of the battle.

The other type of pectorale most commonly in use among the Samnites and other Oscan peoples of south central Italy was the square variety, and it was this variety of pectoral which was later selected for use by the Roman army. This example, now in the British Museum, is south Italian and has been dated to c. 375–325 BC. Note the crude decoration in imitation of human musculature. (Photo: N.V. Sekunda).

nd he is trying to integrate the *accensi*, who as bag-age-carriers would stand behind the whole battle-line, into his account. As he is making the *accensi* combatants, Livy has to invent weapons for them to carry and consequently he has created an entirely spurious five-line formation with three rear lines.

Where we can suggest that the earlier form of the manipular legion differed from that of the second century BC is in the relative importance of the *pilum* and the *hasta*. In his account of the Battle of Beneventum (275 BC) Dionysius writes that 'those who fight in close combat with cavalry spears (i.e. *hastae*) held in the middle with both hands and who frequently achieve success in battle are called *principes* by the Romans'. Now we have good reason to believe that Dionysius' ultimate source at this point was a writer contemporary with the events of the Pyrrhic war, and it may even have been Pyrrhus' own court historian Proxenus. This makes the text unusually reliable and leads to the conclusion that in 275 the *principes* still used a thrusting spear (as the

triarii did even in the mid second century BC) and had not yet converted to the *pilum*. (E. Rawson, 'The Literary Sources for the Pre-Marian Army', *Papers of the British School at Rome* 39 (1971) 13–31.)

In the late fourth century BC, when manipular weapons and tactics were first introduced, it seems that the heavy javelin, later called a *pilum*, was called the *hasta velitaris*, and that the term *hasta* only came to be applied exclusively to the long fighting spear at a later date. Consequently, in the earliest Roman manipular formation, the only line which used the *hasta velitaris* was the first, and these were consequently given the name *hastati* – confusing to us who are more familiar with the later Republican army described by Polybius, in which only the last rank of *triarii* used the *hasta*. Thus in the earliest form of the manipular army only the first line comprising the *hastati* used the *pilum*. The *hastati*, as Dionysius implies, would have been used to break up the enemy formation before the *principes* moved in to secure a final victory with their long spears.

It has been suggested that this mosaic copies an original third century painting. It shows the sacrifice of a pig taking place inside a temple of Mars before a statue of the god. Three priests strike the carcass of the animal with sticks. The scene probably shows the solemnization of an oath of alliance, and the general idea seems to be that if the oath is broken, let the perpetrator be struck down by the god, 'As I strike this pig'. The scene has been compared with a passage in Livy where the carcass of a sacrificed pig is struck with flints rather than sticks. The scene also confirms that a connection existed between swine and the war-god. (Photo: Museo Borghese, Rome)

THE PLATES

A: The Earliest Roman Warriors, c. 700 BC

Had Romulus and Remus existed, they may have looked like these two figures.

A1 uses a helmet and shield based on those found in Esquiline Tomb 94. Tomb 94 also contained fragments of a chariot, including the iron tyres plus nails from the wheels, though these were insufficient to allow a restoration. Fragments of a wooden spear and iron spearhead were also found in Tomb 94, but were too decayed to enable recovery. Consequently the spear shown has been based on an example from Tomb 39 and the pectoral on one from Tomb 86. He carries a short sword of the 'Cuma' type found in Rome. We have no idea what personal dress may have looked like at this period in either Etruria or Latium, so these figures have been given rather coarse clothing decorated with a geometric pattern, as this was the dominating ornamental motif of the time. Whatever the precise form of dress, it would have been secured with bronze *fibulae*, which have been recovered in quantity from a number of the warrior graves. Footwear of this period is a complete mystery. We have restored an ornamental boot of the Etruscan type, although representations of boots of this type with pointed toes are only present in Etruscan art c. 540–475 BC.

A2 uses military equipment entirely based on material from Esquiline findgroup 98, with the exception of the helmet, longsword and scabbard. The helmet is based on that once in the Zschille Collection; the sword an example of 'Rocca di Marro' type from Rome, and the scabbard on material found elsewhere. In the foreground lies an Etruscan warrior based on military equipment found in tombs in Tarquinia. The huts in the background follow a model of the early Iron Age settlement on the Capitoline which was based on the excavated remains of the period.

B: Roman Warrior Bands, seventh century BC

B1 attempts to represent the appearance of a warrior in the seventh century, using the dress recorded for the Salii priests in the later Republican era. The decorated purple tunic known to have been worn by the Salii in the late Republican and Imperial periods may have been somewhat richer than that worn by their warrior predecessors. The cloak (*trabea*) is, in this case, not worn around the shoulders, but is rather worn 'in the Gabinian manner' (*cinctu Gabinus*), in other words rolled up and worn wound around the waist and/or shoulders. This style reputedly spread to Rome from the town of Gabii 12 miles east, which was allied to Rome after 493, though the ultimate origin may have been Etruscan. The cloak has been shown decorated with scarlet stripes and a purple border. The pectoral is based on that from Esquiline Tomb 14 although this is a little early for the seventh century.

B2 attempts to reconstruct the original dress of a *flamen* priest at this period. He wears the pointed

Detail from a red-figure crater in Leipzig dating to the first half of the fourth century, showing a Gallic horseman. Note the straight-bladed Celtic sword and the huge shield. The device painted onto the shield may be that of a particular war-band. The horseman is most probably naked behind the shield. His horse seems to be decorated with some form of body-paint and with bands of phalerae hung around its neck. (Photo: Antikenmuseum, Universität Leipzig)

elmet from which the *apex* supposedly derived, and
the rounded cloak known as a *laena*, of Etruscan
origin but ultimately derived from the Greek cloak
known as a *chlaina*. The priest is dressed in white; the
colour of ritual purity suitable for his office. In later
republican and Imperial times the *flamines* wore a
distinctive boot. The practice of indicating rank by
distinctive shapes and decorative elements in footwear seems to have been Etruscan in origin and to
have spread to Rome. The *flamen* is shown wearing
white boots of a distinctive shape drawn from an
Etruscan statuette.

C: Horatius at the Bridge, 508 BC

Around 509 BC the last Etruscan king, Tarquinius
Superbus, was expelled from Rome and appealed to
the king of Clusium, Lars Porsenna, who may also
have been head of the Etruscan League at this time,
to restore him to the Roman throne. Porsenna
marched on Rome and seized the Janiculum in a
sudden attack; the way lay open to the rest of the city
across the Tiber. Livy records a story that Horatius
Cocles rushed to the bridge, together with Spurius
Larcius and Titus Herminius, and together the three
held back the whole Etruscan army, while behind
them work continued feverishly on the demolition of
the bridge. When scarcely anything was left of the
bridge Horatius sent back the two others and carried
on the fight alone. With a crash and a deafening shout
from the Romans the bridge finally fell. Horatius
invoked Father Tiber, leaped into the river, and
swam to the bank and safety.

The three figures are based on polychrome representations of hoplites dating to the late sixth or
early fifth centuries BC.

C1 is based on a fragment from the central
acroterium of the Sassi Caduti temple at Falerii
Veteres, and so represents an Etruscan hoplite of the
period.

C2 is based on the painted terracotta body of an
Amazon from the pediment of a temple on the
Esquiline hill. It is highly debatable whether this
decorated fragment can be taken as an accurate
reflection of the dress of a Roman warrior of the early
fifth century. The style and decoration of the cuirass
is of a type normally found specifically on representations of Amazons, and is not really appropriate for a
male Roman warrior. Furthermore the sculpture is of

This Roman gold stater, dating to 218 BC, shows on its reverse Italian and Roman generals swearing an oath of alliance over a pig (J.P.C. Kent and Max and Albert Hirmer, Roman Coins (1978) no. 14, pl. 7). Note the muscle–cuirass worn by the Roman general, and the decorative point to his lance, which may be a badge of his rank. (Photo: Hirmer Fotoarchiv, München)

Greek workmanship, and the representational style is
clearly Greek. Nevertheless we have incorporated
the sculpture within this plate, in order to use all
sources of representational evidence in colour for the
period.

C3 is based on a fragment of a fictile plaque from the
temple of Mater Matuta in Satricum. Latin hoplites
are not known to have fought as allies of Lars
Porsenna, but he is known to have used mercenary
troops. One piece of evidence for this is the story of
Mucius Scaevola who attempted to assassinate the
Etruscan king in his camp, but by mistake killed the
king's scribe, who was paying out money to the
army.

D: The Venetic Fighting System, fifth century BC

This plate is based on the figures from the Certosa
Situla, representing the various components of the
Venetic battle-line. As it would not be practicable to
depict full scale maniples in any detail, we have
shown the troop types as four single advancing lines.

The reconstruction of the shield of **D1** has not

been straightforward, as it is impossible to tell whether the main body of the shield shown is intended to be non-metallic, with only the rim and boss in bronze, or whether the whole shield is supposed to be covered in a bronze facing. Similarly with **D2** it is not clear whether the shields are non-metallic or covered in bronze sheeting. Here we have followed Peter Connolly in showing the shields as non-metallic but with bronze bosses.

D3 has been shown with bronze hoplite shields. In the sixth century the Greek hoplite shield had a bronze rim, a bronze internal vertical handle for the elbow, and sometimes a bronze shield device attached to the front. The rest of the shield consisted of multiple layers of ox-hide. At the turn of the century,

at a date which cannot be specified precisely, the entire shield becomes faced with a thin bronze sheet stressed to give it strength. Thus we cannot be sure whether we should show these Venetic warriors with bronze-faced shields or not. These Venetic shields seem to be of local manufacture – the triangular decoration of the shield-rim is in stark contrast to the multiple cable pattern found on the overwhelming majority of hoplite shields manufactured on the Greek mainland. We have also given these hoplites bronze greaves, although these are not shown on the situla.

D4 represents the group of Venetic axemen shown on the Certosa Situla. The precise details of the cuirass cannot be worked out from the situla, and we have interpreted the cuirass as being of different coloured heavy linen or other textile material, not unlike the Greek *spolas*. The situla as a whole conveys the impression that there was some standardization of dress and equipment, but this is surely just an artistic device. It is difficult to believe that there was anything approaching state issue of equipment and uniformity of dress among the Veneti at a date as early as this.

E: Roman Hoplites defeated by Celts, fourth century BC
During the fourth century central Italy, including Latium, was subjected to periodic invasions by Gallic tribes. This plate depicts the rout of a Roman army during one of these battles.

E1 is based on the fourth century ivory plaques from Praeneste, **E2** is based on the François Tomb and **E3** is based on the cist in St Petersburg. The uniformity

Fragment of a tomb-painting from the Esquiline possibly copying one of the series of historical frescoes painted by Fabius Pictor to decorate the Temple of Salus in 304. The Samnite general (left) is labelled as Marcus Fannius, the Roman as Q. Fabius; perhaps Q. Fabius Maximus Rullianus, dictator in 315. The scene may, therefore, represent the surrender of a Samnite city during this year. The Samnite wears a Montefortino helmet with 'wing' plumes at the side (pennae), a goat-skin cloak, a white subligaculum (lion-cloth) and two greaves, and carries a huge oval shield. The Roman general is shown carrying a long fighting hasta as a badge of his office, and is draped in his cloak (paludamentum). Behind him his cohors praetoria is drawn up, carrying long hastae and dressed in white tunics, as was the practice in later Roman armies.

Two details taken from a Praenestine situla in Berlin. The situla as a whole shows a scene of sacrifice, attended by a Roman general carrying an eagle-standard, and a member of his entourage carrying a lituus; a badge of office of Etruscan origin. The lituus-bearer wears boots with ornamental folded-down tops, perhaps precursors of those worn by members of the equestrian order, and a pair of greaves. (Photo: Berlin, Staatliche Museen)

of the muscle-cuirasses and greaves is remarkable, and can perhaps be taken as evidence for at least some kind of standardization of military equipment within the Roman hoplite army in the fourth century. The red colour of the tunics is taken from the François Tomb painting. The shield device of **E2**, the head of a minotaur, is based on an Etruscan mirror, but the 'legionary' shield blazons of the other figures are loosely based on Republican coinage. The fourth century archaeological sources on which these figures are based invariably show Latin hoplites clean-shaven, which is something of a paradox, as tradition maintained that the first barbers only came to Rome in the third century BC.

E4 is based on a red-figure crater in Leipzig, while **E5** is based on a third century wall painting from the Esquiline, now in the Palazzo dei Conservatori, Rome.

F: Samnite Warriors, c. 293 BC
This plate attempts a reconstruction of the dress which might have been worn by the Samnite army at the Battle of Aquilonia in 293.

F1 attempts to reconstruct the appearance of a soldier of the *legio linteata*. All his weapons and dress are either whitened or silvered. The cuirass is based on the Bardo cuirass, while the helmet (note the crest, mentioned by Livy) and the greave repeat the same decorative motifs found on the cuirass.

F2, together with various figures in the background, represents the balance of the Samnite army, dressed in their 'parti-coloured' tunics. The Samnite tunic was extremely short and curved at the bottom, so as to cover the genitalia, and had short sleeves, like a modern T-shirt. Bands of decorated material were applied at the shoulder, sleeves, hem, chest, etc., as in these examples, which are based on paintings of warriors from Paestan tombs and Lucanian vases. The decorative colours and motifs have been repeated on the shields. Whether their arms were truly gilded, or whether this is a hyperbole (for bronze weapons) of Livy or of his source, is not known. Some warriors carry spears, and some carry javelins based on the Vulci javelin.

G: Sacrifice establishing a treaty between Romans and Samnites
The central and background scene in this plate is based on the mosaic in the Museo Borghese depicting a sacrifice held before Mars.

G1 and **G2** are based on two figures from a Praenestine situla in Berlin. Both wear olive wreaths,

This oval shield, shown on a Roman aes signatum coin of five Roman pounds which was struck about 280 BC, is presumably of the type carried by the Roman legionary of the period. There remains the possibility, however, that it may be shown as an item of booty.

A second example of Roman bronze bar coinage, also struck in the early third century, shows a sword and a scabbard with baldric, both of distinctively Greek type. Again the equipment shown is presumably Roman, and if so this coin confirms that the Spanish sword had not yet been adopted by the Roman army.

probably symbols of victory in this context, which may be taken as an indication that the general is a *triumphator* celebrating his triumph, which would, in turn, explain his extremely complex dress. The literary sources are somewhat confused as to whether and under what circumstances Roman generals wore crimson or scarlet, which has made the reconstruction of the colours for these two figures somewhat problematical. We have in the end decided on scarlet with heavy gold embroidery. The general wears a cloak with a border measuring a palm's width, heavily embroidered in gold.

52 is based on the figure of the Samnite general Marcus Fannius from a historical painting found in a tomb on the Esquiline.

4: Roman Hastati *fight one of Pyrrhus' elephants*

The Epirote war elephant is based on a contemporary representation of an elephant and its calf on a painted plate now in the Museo Nazionale di Villa Giulia. It is clear from the painting that the crew wear muscle-cuirasses (the naveal is quite clear on the driver's cuirass). Their tunics, as well as the housing of the elephant, are dark crimson. The helmets have a triple plume, most probably of white horsehair. The yellow-painted tower on the elephant's back (presum-ably wooden) is protected on each side by a bronze hoplite shield, and is held in place by three thick chains.

The elephant is shown in conflict with a maniple of Roman *hastati*. The *hastati* are shown without muscle-cuirass, coat of mail, or *pectorale*. The tendency seems to have been for the *manipularii* of all three ranks to have become progressively more heavily equipped as time passed; thus in the late Republic all *manipularii* wore coats of mail. The Roman troops wear Montefortino helmets, and carry swords and shields based on *aes grave* coins. They have been supplied with a single greave on the leading leg, which has been based on those worn by the *lituus*-bearer shown on a Praenestine situla.

The legionaries of the Roman Imperial army are known to have worn tunics of a natural off-white colour. This 'uniformly' drab appearance may well have come about in the Roman army following its massive expansion in the middle of the fourth century, the mass of new Roman warriors repeatedly pressed into service choosing to clothe themselves in the cheapest undyed cloth. For similar reasons of cost the rapidly expanding armies of the Bourbon and Hapsburg monarchies adopted uniform clothing in cheap natural colours at the end of the 17th century of our era.

Locri had at first supported Pyrrhus, but, when Rome confirmed her independence after the defeat of Pyrrhus, she declared her loyalty to Rome on this coin, struck c. 274. Pistis 'loyalty' is here shown crowning Roma. Note the oval shield, with rim, spine and boss, used by Roma. This archaeological evidence confirms that the scutum was used by the Roman army by this date, and also gives us its precise size and appearance. (Photo: N.V. Sekunda)

Notes sur les planches en couleur

A Les premiers guerriers Romains vers 700 avant J.C. Si Romulus et Rémus avaient existé, ils auraient bien pu ressembler à ces deux personnages. Al utilise du matériel basé sur les objets retrouvés dans la tombe 94 du Mont Esquilin. Il porte un court glaive du type 'Cuma' retrouvé à Rome. Nous ne possédons aucune information quant aux costumes. Ces personnages ont donc été vêtus de manière assez grossière et leurs vêtements sont agrémentés d'un motif géométrique. **A2** utilise du matériel militaire basé entièrement sur les objets du Groupe 98 du Mont Esquilin, sauf pour le casque, le glaive et le fourreau.

B Bandes de guerriers Romains, Septième siècle avant J.C. La planche B1 tente de représenter un guerrier au septième siècle, en s'inspirant du costume mentionné pour les prêtres Salii durant la période républicaine plus tardive. La cape se porte roulée et autour de la taille et/ou des épaules. Elle est agrémentée de rayures écarlates et bordée de pourpre. **B2** tente de reconstituer le costume original d'un prêtre *flamen* de cette époque. Il porte un casque à pointe et une cape arrondie.

C Horace au Pont 508 avant J.C. Tite-Live raconte l'histoire de la défense dü pont par Horace qui, avec Spurius, Larcius et Titus Herminius, réussirent à tenir en respect toute l'armée étrusque alors que d'autres tentaient fiévreusement de démolir le pont, qui finit par s'effondrer. Horace invoqua le dieu du Tibre, plongea et traversa à la nage pour se retrouver sur l'autre rive sain et sauf.

D Le Système de combat des Vénètes (cinquième siècle avant J.C.). Cette planche s'inspire de figures de la Situle Certosa, représentant divers éléments de la ligne de combat des Vénètes. **D1** La reconstitution du bouclier ne fut pas simple. Comme pour **D2**, on ne sait pas si les boucliers étaient non-métalliques ou s'ils étaient recouverts d'une feuille de bronze. Ici, nous avons représenté les boucliers comme étant non-métalliques mais avec un ombon en bronze. **D3** comporte des boucliers hoplite en bronze. Nous avons également donné à ces hoplites des cnémides de bronze bien qu'elles n'apparaissent pas sur la situle. Nous avons interprété la cuirasse comme étant constituée de lin épais de couleurs différentes ou autre textile.

E Hoplites Romains vaincus par des Celtes (quatrième siècle avant J.C.). Au quatrième siècle, les tribus Galliques envahissaient de temps à autre le centre de l'Italie, y compris le Latium. Cette planche dépeint la déroute d'une armée romaine durant l'un de ses combats. L'uniformité des cuirasses et des cnémides est remarquable. On peut peut-être en conclure qu'il existait un certain degré de standardisation du matériel militaire dans l'armée romaine hoplite au quatrième siècle.

F Guerriers Samnites vers 293 avant J.C. Cette planche tente de reconstituer l'uniforme qui aurait pu être porté par l'armée Samnite à la bataille d'Aquilona en 293. **F1** tente de restituer l'apparence d'un soldat de la *legio linteata*. **F2**, ainsi que diverses figures en arrière-plan, représente le reste de l'armée Samnite, vêtue de tuniques 'multicolores'. Les couleurs et motifs décoratifs ont été repris sur les boucliers.

G Sacrifice établissant un traité entre les Romains et les Samnites. G1 et G3 se sont inspirés de deux personnages d'une situle de Préneste qui se trouve à Berlin. Le général est un *triumphator* qui fête son triomphe, ce qui explique la complexité de son costume. Il porte une cape lourdement brodée d'or. G2 s'inspire du personnage du général Samnite Marcus Fannius sur une fresque historique retrouvée dans une tombe du Mont Esquilin.

H Les *Hastati* Romains se mesurent à l'un des éléphants de Pyrrhus. L'éléphant guerrier épirote s'inspire de la représentation contemporaine d'un éléphant et de son éléphanteau sur une assiette peinte qui se trouve aujourd'hui au Museo Nazionale di Villa Giulia. Les membres de l'équipage portent une cuirasse et une tunique écarlate foncé. L'éléphant est représenté en conflit avec un manipule de *Hastati* Romains sans cuirasse, cotte de mailles ou *pectorale*. Ils portent le casque Nontefortino et ont un bouclier et un glaive qui s'inspirent des pièces de monnaie *aes grave*. On leur a fourni une seule cnémide, sur la jambe d'appel.

Farbtafeln

A Frührömische Soldaten ca. 700 vor Christi Geburt. Wenn Romulus und Remᵘ tatsächlich gelebt hätten, hätten sie wohl wie die zwei hier abgebildeten Soldate ausgesehen. Die Ausrüstung von A1 basiert auf der, die in Grab 94 auf de Esquilin gefunden wurde. Der Soldat trägt ein in Rom gefundenes Kurzschwe des Typs 'Cuma'. Es gibt keine Anhaltspunkte für die persönlichen Kleider, uᵣ die Figuren tragen daher ziemlich derbe, mit geometrischen Mustern verzierᵗ Kleider. Die Ausrüstung von A2 basiert ganz auf Gegenständen, die beim Fund auf dem Esquilin gefunden wurden, mit Ausnahme des Helms, des Langschwertᵉ und der Schwertscheide.

B Römische Soldatengruppe, 7. Jahrhundert vor Christi Geburt. B1 stellt eineᵣ Versuch dar, gestützt auf die Kleider der salischen Priester aus dᵉ republikanischen Zeit einen Soldaten aus dem 7. Jahrhundert darzustellen. Dᵉ Mantel wird aufgerollt um die Hüften und/oder die Schultern getragen. Er ist mᵢ scharlachroten Streifen und einem purpurnen Saum verziert. B2 stellt eineᵣ Rekonstruktionsversuch der Kleider der Flamen dieser Zeit dar. Er trägt eineᵣ Spitzhelm und einen runden Mantel.

C Horatius an der Brücke, 508 vor Christi Geburt. Livius erzählt die Geschichᵗ der Verteidigung der Brücke durch Horatius, Spurius Larcius und Tit Herminius, die zusammen die ganze etruskische Armee aufhielten, während andeᵣ Soldaten eiligst die Brücke abbrachen. Die Brücke stürzte schließlich ein. Horatiᵘ beschwor den Vater Tiber, sprang in den Fluß und schwamm ans andere Ufer Sicherheit.

D Die venetische Schlachtordnung (5. Jahrhundert vor Christi Geburt). Diesᵉ Tafel basiert auf Abbildungen auf der Certosa Situla, die verschiedene Teile dᵉ venetischen Schlachtordnung darstellen. D1 Es handelt sich um eine annäherᵈ Rekonstruktion des Schildes. Auch bei D2 ist nicht klar, ob die Schilde nicht aᵘ Metall sind oder mit Bronze beschlagen sind. Die hier abgebildeten Schilde sinᵈ nicht aus Metall, weisen jedoch Bronzeverzierung auf. D3 stellt einen Bronzeschild eines Hopliten dar. Wir haben den Hopliten auch Beinschienen aᵘ Bronze gegeben, obwohl diese auf der Situla nicht abgebildet sind. D4 stellt eineᵣ Gruppe venetischer Soldaten mit Axten dar, wie sie auf der Certosa Situ abgebildet sind. Wir nehmen an, daß der Küraß aus mehrfarbiger schwerer Leiᵣ oder aus anderen Textilien bestand.

E Niederlage römischer Hopliten gegen die Kelten (4. Jahrhundert vor Chrisᵗ Geburt). Während des vierten vorchristlichen Jahrhunderts war Mittelitaliᵉ einschließlich Latiums, periodischen Invasionen durch keltische Stämmᵉ ausgesetzt. Diese Tafel stellt die Vernichtung einer römischen Armee währeᵈ einer dieser Schlachten dar. Zu beachten ist die erstaunliche Uniformität deᵣ Muskel-Kürasse und Beinschienen, sie gibt einen Hinweis auf den Grad dᵉ Vereinheitlichung militärischer Ausrüstungen der Hopliten des viertᵉᵣ vorchristlichen Jahrhunderts.

F Samnitische Soldaten, ca. 293 vor Christi Geburt. Diese Tafel ist eiᵣ Rekonstruktionsversuch der Kleider, die von samnitischen Soldaten während dᵉ Schlacht von Aquilona im Jahr 293 vor Christi Geburt getragen wurden. F1 ist eiᵣ Rekonstruktionsversuch eines Soldaten der Legio linteate. F2 sowie dᵢ verschiedenen Abbildungen im Hintergrund stellen den Rest der samnitischeᵣ Armee in ihren farbig verzierten Tuniken dar. Die Farben und Motive dᵉ Verzierungen sind auch auf den Schilden zu finden.

G Opfer zum Abschluß eines Vertrages zwischen den Römern und Samnitern. Gᵢ und G3 basieren auf zwei Abbildungen auf einer pränestinischen Situla, die sich Berlin befindet. Der General ist ein Triumphator, der seinen Sieg feiert, und isᵗ darum derart reich gekleidet. Er trägt einen goldverzierten Mantel. G2 basiert aᵘ einer Abbildung des samnitischen Generals Marcus Fannius auf einem altᵉ Gemälde, das in einem Grab auf dem Esquilin gefunden wurde.

H Römische Hastati im Kampf mit einem Elefanten von Pyrrhus. Der epirotischᵉ Kriegselefant basiert auf einer zeitgenössischen Darstellung eines Elefanten mᵢ seinem Jungen auf einer Tafel, die sich heute im Museo Nazionale di Villa Giuli befindet. Die Reiter tragen Muskel-Kürasse und scharlachrote Tuniken. Dᵉ Elefant ist im Kampf mit einem Manipel römischer Hastati verwickelt. Diesᵉ tragen Montefortino-Helme und Schwerter und Schilde, die auf den Aes graveᵣ Münzen basieren. sie tragen eine Beinschiene am vorgestellten Bein.